LIFEGAMES
ACTIVITY-CENTERED LEARNING FOR EARLY CHILDHOOD EDUCATION IN ECONOMICS

SAUL Z. BARR

University of Tennessee at Martin

▲ Addison-Wesley Publishing Company

Menlo Park, California • Reading, Massachusetts
London • Amsterdam • Don Mills, Ontario • Sydney

ABOUT THE AUTHOR

Dr. Saul Z. Barr, associate professor of economics at the University of Tennessee at Martin, has had a particular interest in the teaching of economics to children in the primary grades. In that capacity he helped design over 75 lessons for the "Romper Room" television program that reached over two million preschoolers per day. This, a first in television economics for preschoolers, was the inspiration for this K–3 source book.

Dr. Barr was formerly the director of the Maryland Council on Economic Education at Towson State University. Later, he was director of the Stamford Center for Economic Education at the University of Connecticut, where he held the academic rank of associate professor of economics. Over the years he has helped design curricula for schools in Georgia, Maryland, Michigan, and Connecticut. He has published reviews and research articles in *The Journal of Economic Education, The Journal of Business Education, The Southern Economics Journal,* and others. Numerous sessions on the teaching of economics have been chaired by him at national conferences, and he has delivered papers on economics education at meetings of the Southern Economics Association, the Eastern Economics Association, and the annual convention of the National Council for the Social Studies, where he is a member of the Educational Publishers Committee.

This book is published by the Addison-Wesley Innovative Division.

The blackline masters in this publication are designed to be used with appropriate duplicating equipment to reproduce copies for classroom use. Addison-Wesley Publishing Company grants permission to classroom teachers to reproduce these masters.

Copyright © 1985 by Addison-Wesley Publishing Company, Inc. All rights reserved. Printed in the United States of America. Published simultaneously in Canada.

ISBN 0-201-20094-5   ABCDEFGHIJKL-ML-8987654

DEDICATION

Dedicated to Helga Rachel Barr and Sara Emilia Barr for creating the atmosphere for learning about the world of children.

ACKNOWLEDGMENTS

Special thanks to the teachers and curriculum supervisors who helped me know the importance of economics understanding for young children. Thanks also to Sally Gelbart of Romper Room Enterprises in Towson, Maryland, for the opportunity to be the originator of over 75 segments in economics for television. Peggy Powell, the former director of programming, taught me much about how to reach children with short, innovative activities. I also thank the staff of the Maryland Council on Economic Education.

The photographs in this book were taken at Sherman Elementary School in San Francisco, California. Many thanks to Miss Rachelle Reyes and her class of first grade students, for being so helpful.

S.Z.B.

CONTENTS

Introduction

How *Lifegames* Begins the Study of Economics vii
The Development of Economic Learning through *Lifegames* viii
What Children Will Learn about Economics ix

Section One: Goods and Services (List of Lessons and Main Themes) 1

1 Pictures 2
2 Lost Child 4
3 Show and Tell 6
4 Wild Animal 8
5 Circle Game 10
6 Hats and Shoes 12
7 The Raft, Part 1 (Shelter) 14
8 The Raft, Part 2 (Food and Water) 16
9 The Raft, Part 3 (Clothing) 18
10 Will It Last? 20
11 I Wish I May, I Wish I Might! 22
12 This Is What I Want 24
13 The Best Choice 26
14 Sports Station 28
15 Baseball Jobs 30
16 Listen and Do 32
17 Spelling Blocks 34
18 Shopping in the Newspaper 36
19 Spelling Soccer 38
20 Can of Peas 40

Section Two: Specialization and Jobs (List of Lessons and Main Themes) 43

1 Airplanes 44
2 Jobs and Tools 46
3 Police Officer, Baker, Firefighter, Farmer, and Teacher 48
4 Help Wanted: Circus 50
5 Let's Go Fishing 52
6 What My Mom and Dad Do 54
7 Bread Line 56
8 Library 58
9 Whispers 60
10 Charades 62
11 The Crayon Box 64
12 Jobs Help Us 66
13 Occupation Rummy 68
14 Paperweights 70
15 Help Wanted 72
16 Which Job Is Best for Me? 74
17 Building a Home 76
18 Public Service Jobs (Government) 78
19 Labor Unions 80
20 Classified Ads 82

Section Three: Resources (List of Lessons and Main Themes) 85

1 Factors of Production 86
2 Salvage Game 88
3 Resource Match 90
4 The Big Tree 92
5 The Vacant Lot 94
6 Some Grow Back 96
7 Farms and Factories 98
8 Our Town 100
9 Animals 102
10 Labor 104
11 Capital 106
12 Management 108
13 The Maze 110
14 American Indians' Resources 112
15 The Globe 114
16 Resource Match 116
17 Building a House 118
18 Education 120
19 Stickers 122
20 Family 124

Section Four: Money and the Bank (List of Lessons and Main Themes) 127

1 Big Nickel, Little Dime 128
2 The One-dollar Bill 130
3 Bill-matching Game 132
4 Spending a Dollar 134
5 Money Math 136
6 Heads—You Win! 138
7 Dogs 140
8 Barter/Trade 142
9 Vegetable Money 144
10 The Bank 146
11 Shopping Spree 148
12 Money Math Is for Me! 150
13 Checks 152
14 Green Card, Red Card 154
15 Crayon Money 156
16 Money Madness 158
17 Make a Deal 160
18 Why Prices? 162
19 Around the World 164
20 Jobs and Money 166

Glossary of Economic Terms 168

Blackline Masters 172

INTRODUCTION

How *Lifegames* Begins the Study of Economics

The study of economics in the social studies curriculum is relatively new. Even at the college level economics was not taught extensively until the mid-1940s. Recently more and more private and public school systems have begun developing strategies for teaching economics in grades K–12. Many states have gone so far as to mandate the teaching of economics through the integration of economics concepts in K–12.[1] More than half of our states have such a mandate. To serve this great need, *Lifegames* has been designed to fit easily into the existing K–3 social studies curriculum. Each section as well as each of the eighty lessons is self-contained; blackline masters are provided at the end of the book for the completion of some activities. Most lessons can be used with both readers and non-readers, and only very basic mathematics skills are required. The lessons build on basic math and reading skills. As the lessons reinforce these skills, they also provide simple ways of introducing the most widely mandated economic concepts. A glossary of economic terms is included for easy reference.

Children learn from the world around them, i.e., about life; thus, this book for them is called *Lifegames*. In a sense, life in our world is based on many economic relationships. Section One introduces the children to the basic function of society as the provider of goods and services. Society is charged by individuals to organize production of goods and services for our survival. Children begin to recognize goods, services, and the means by which they are produced. Section Two describes specialization and jobs. Children learn that in order to produce enough to satisfy a growing economy, people must specialize in the jobs they do. The child's world is expanded into a world of many exciting professions. Children begin to understand why parents work inside and outside the home. Section Three describes resources, since resources are fundamental to a growing economy. Nothing can or will be produced or consumed without the necessary resources. Children learn that resources from land are combined with capital and labor and are organized by management to produce the needs of society. Section Four on money and banking brings to day-to-day reality many of the concepts learned. Children learn the meaning of money and its value.

[1] Brennan, Dennis C. and Ronald A. Banaszak. *A Study of State Mandates and Competencies for Economics Education.* Stockton, CA: Center for the Development of Economics Education, 1982.

The purpose of banking is shown as they deal with having their own classroom savings and checking accounts. Children are taught what money looks like, how to identify different denominations of coin and paper money, and how to trade for goods and services with money. Even though lessons can be used individually, when they *all* are used they provide a complete introduction to the operation of an economy.

Teachers should note that care has been taken to insure that concepts introduced conform with the Master Curriculum Guide for Our Nation's Schools, published by the Joint Council on Economic Education,[2] as well as the conceptual format of many state, county, and district curriculum guides. Teachers are encouraged to review the section on concepts to see that *Lifegames* satisfies their individual curriculum needs.

The Development of Economic Learning through *Lifegames*

All societies are faced with the same problem—allocating scarce resources to various uses. Every society must find some organized way of choosing how scarce resources are to be used. This organized selection is a society's economic system.

Any economic system must answer four basic questions.
1. What goods and services shall be produced? A system of priorities must be established, because a society cannot produce everything it wants.
2. How shall these goods and services be produced? Different mixes of the factors of production (land, labor, capital, and managerial skills) can be utilized to produce the same product.
3. How much will be produced in total? What will the growth rate be, and how can we keep production stable to avoid job losses and uncertain prices?
4. Who shall receive the goods and services produced? What process can be used to decide who gets what? Either goods and services can be sold in

---

[2]For more information, contact the Joint Council on Economic Education, 2 Park Ave., New York, NY 10016.

a marketplace to whomever can earn the income to pay for them, or some ruler or rulers could decide for us.

These questions in our society form a sound basis for the introduction of economic social studies in understanding one's role in the family, community, and society as a whole. These basic questions are intertwined throughout the eighty lessons in *Lifegames.*

At the preschool and primary levels, children can relate to those goods and services they have encountered in their lives. Children have already experienced people in a wide variety of job activities and have seen people use many and varied resources. Children have had numerous occasions to see what money can be used for. The four main concepts, therefore, that *Lifegames* covers are goods and services, specialization and jobs, resources, and money and banking. As each set of activities is done, children will begin to see the relationships going on around them daily in the supermarket, drugstore, barbershop, or amusement park: people working with people in our economy.

What Children Will Learn about Economics

Section One: *Goods:* Understanding the process of producing things we need and seeing
Goods and how and why they are produced is essential for the early development of
Services children's economic understanding. Once children have begun to perceive the items around them they will begin to realize the importance of the system that produces these goods.

Teachers should realize that businesses produce most goods but that some are produced by the government. Goods are produced for both personal consumption and business consumption for future production.

Children will first identify the items they consume. Later it will be easier for them to recognize goods involved in the production of other goods.

Services: Our wants for services, like those for goods, are unlimited. These wants sometimes go far beyond our ability to satisfy them. Children will find the understanding of an intangible, such as services, more difficult. After the concept of a good has been explained and reinforced, services will become easier to understand. More than 50 percent of working Americans are involved in providing services. Children should begin to realize the services they and their families use and perform.

Goods and Services: People are both producers and consumers. In our occupations we produce goods and services and use the income thus derived to purchase other goods and services.

Teachers will begin to differentiate for the class what kinds of goods and services are produced. Children will learn that government and businesses provide goods and services. Questions will begin to rise in children's minds about what should be produced, how it would be produced, and for whom it should be produced. These questions will begin to have answers as the activities proceed.

Section Two: Specialization and Jobs

In the evolution of the American economic system, which is primarily private enterprise, we have sought increased efficiency in the production of goods and services to increase our standard of living. Thus we have become more specialized in what we do. By having each individual specialize in one task, each becomes more proficient at his or her task, and the society benefits in more ways.

With the reinforcing exercises in *Lifegames,* children will be able to perform dozens of tasks. With these tasks will come a basic understanding of different specialties (e.g., police officer, baker, firefighter, teacher, etc.), and the children will begin to see how each of us is dependent on the others to produce the goods and services we need. For example, children will learn that the pilot depends on the farmer and the police officer, and the police officer depends on the merchant and the gardener; in a sense we all work for each other in our economy.

Section Three: Resources

Understanding how goods and services are produced though specialized jobs will open children's minds to resources. Because available resources are insufficient to satisfy everybody's wants for goods and services, some very serious choices need to be made. Resources can be saved for the future or used today.

The activities in this section highlight the items children use. The many and varied resources that go into products are learned. The major categories of resources are land and water, people or labor, machines and money or capital, and the management of each. Resources are combined to make goods and services. For example, land yields trees, which can be turned into lumber by people using machines under the supervision of managers. Children will learn how resources are used in the production of goods and services.

Section Four: Money and the Bank

Money is printed in a controlled amount by the government. It provides us with a medium for the exchange of goods and services, a way to store the value or wealth we have accrued, and a yardstick to measure the value of things we produce. Money is a convenience that simplifies economic exchanges.

The amount of money in our total system changes from year to year. Sometimes it grows very fast compared to how fast output of goods and services is growing. For instance, in one activity children will trade whatever amount of crayons they happen to have for raisins. Trading will cause the number of crayons needed to increase to a point at which most children will be able to buy at least one box of raisins. Children will have the opportunity to use as many crayons as they can the next day to trade for raisins. As you can imagine, the children may want to use hundreds of crayons and soon may be trading many more crayons for raisins than they did the previous day. In this way children will begin to see that there is a relationship between the amount of money in a system and prices of things.

Banks will be introduced as places where we get services for our money. The idea of money growing in a savings account will be introduced, as well as the meaning of a check or credit card. Children will have a chance to play games that stimulate buying, selling, saving, and borrowing in many different ways.

As you can see, the four sections in *Lifegames,* even though each is self-contained, provide a continuum of learning about economic social studies. Each section in sequence can be used to build on the previous section, until the children begin to understand more about the real world around them. You may want to use some of these activities with other areas of instruction in your classroom. Many activities can be used with individual children at work stations, or with the entire class.

Young children come to preschools and primary grades well prepared to begin learning about the world around them. The problem, however, is how to harness youngsters' tremendous curiosity about the real world, and their natural ability to play to create an effective learning environment. *Lifegames* gives children that opportunity.

SECTION ONE
GOODS AND SERVICES

lesson	main theme	page
1 Pictures	Goods	2
2 Lost Child	Services	4
3 Show and Tell	Goods at home	6
4 Wild Animal	Food as a good	8
5 Circle Game	Goods versus services	10
6 Hats and Shoes	Business and government services	12
7 The Raft, Part 1 (Shelter)	Necessities	14
8 The Raft, Part 2 (Food and Water)	The four food groups as necessities	16
9 The Raft, Part 3 (Clothing)	Clothing as a necessity	18
10 Will It Last?	Durable versus nondurable goods	20
11 I Wish I May, I Wish I Might!	Free goods from nature	22
12 This Is What I Want	Consumer and producer	24
13 The Best Choice	Value of a good or service	26
14 Sports Station	Sports goods	28
15 Baseball Jobs	Tools used by producers	30
16 Listen and Do	Goods and services in songs	32
17 Spelling Blocks*	Spelling goods and services	34
18 Shopping in the Newspaper*	Math skills in comparison shopping	36
19 Spelling Soccer*	Spelling goods and services	38
20 Can of Peas*	Judging value by size, quality, usefulness, and price	40

*For students who are readers and can write simple sentences.

Pictures

Objectives	Learning to identify a good in a picture as something that can be owned and held and taken home; learning to make presentations.
Activity	The children are told stories about pictures in magazines. Children decide which pictures are of goods. This exercise is repeated until each child knows what a good is.
Getting Started	Each child is given an old magazine and a pair of scissors and asked to cut out "a pretty picture." After you collect all the pictures, pick one out and ask, "Who cut out this one of a _____? Did you think this was pretty? Why?" If it was a picture of a house, you may want to say, "Here is a picture of a house. Inside there may be a family just like yours." Tell the class a story about the picture. You may want to give individual children an opportunity to describe the picture they have cut out. After telling the children that a good is something they can own, hold, and take home with them and is sometimes sold in stores, ask them to take any one of the pictures you are holding and circle the goods. Give each child an opportunity to explain what they have done and why each circled item is a good.
Follow-up Discussion	Is there anything in the picture you have? Does your mother or father have anything in your picture? Would you like to have the good in your picture? Where would you get a good like that, and where would you keep it?
Materials	Old magazines. Scissors. Crayons.

2 Lost Child

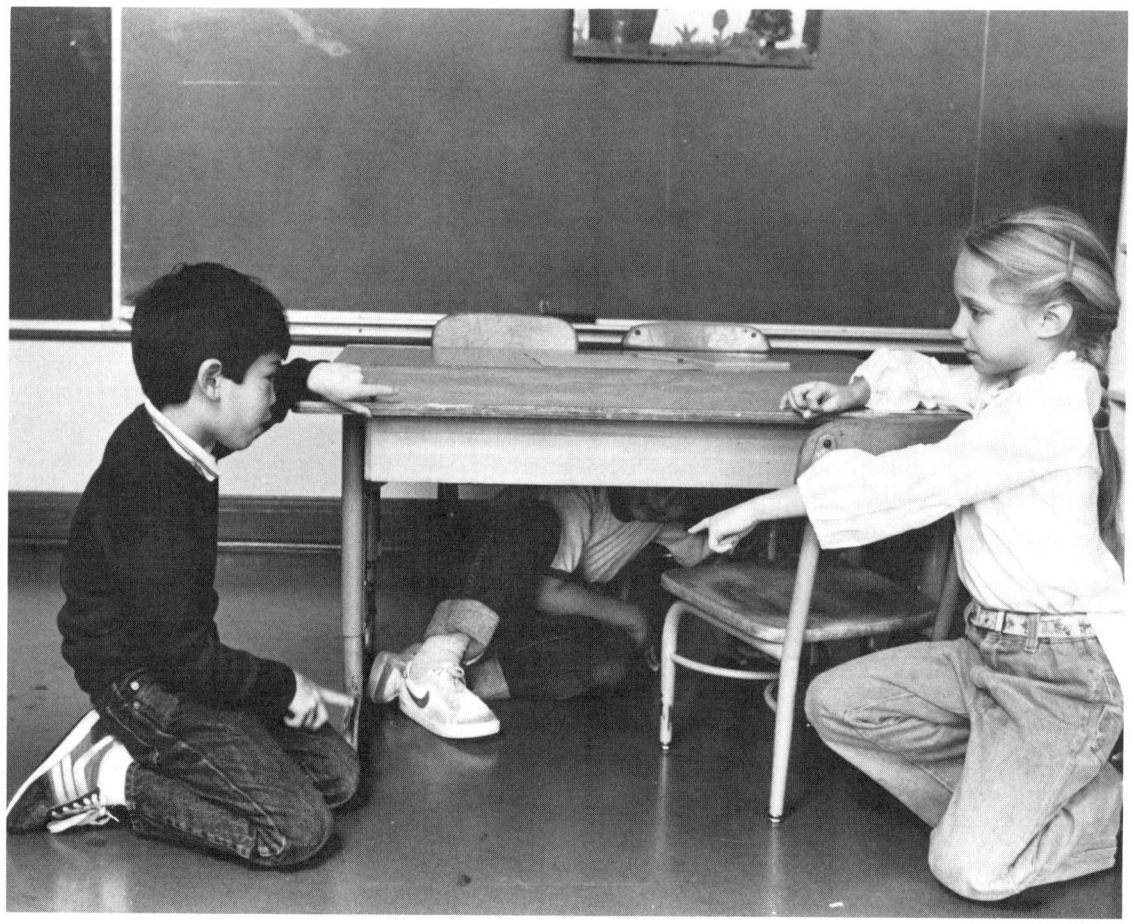

Objectives	Understanding the meaning of a service as something one does for the benefit of someone else; group interaction skills; leadership skills.
Activity	A child is selected at random by the teacher to hide in the classroom while the remainder of the children put their heads down on their desks and cover their eyes. After the child is "lost," four children are selected to organize a search. When the lost child is found, the leader of the group is asked how it was done.
Getting Started	The teacher might ask, "Do you know where the lost child is?" The teacher could ask those in the search party to explain whether they were offering a good or a service to the lost child and those who would want the child back. The teacher might ask, "What did you do for the lost child? Why did that mean something for the lost child and the class? Why is what you did a service?" The teacher should also explore who in the community searches for lost children and why police officers are important friends.
Follow-up Discussion	Can you name other services? What other things do police officers do? What do firefighters do? What do plumbers do? What do pilots do? What do bus drivers do? What service does your teacher give? What services do you give? What services do members of your family give?

3 Show and Tell

6   Goods and Services

Objectives	Understanding goods that are in the home.
Activity	Children are told to bring into school something that is used a great deal by them or other members of their families at home. Instruct them *not* to bring in toys.
Getting Started	Have the children explain why they brought the good they did. The teacher, for example, might want to ask a child who brought in a bar of soap, "Why did you bring in soap? Is soap a good? Show me at the sink what you do with it. Why is soap important to everyone in your family?"
Follow-up Discussion	Goods that provide cleanliness or nutrition may provide introductions to discussions. Where do you keep your goods? Do you have your own? Where in the home did your good come from? Have children exchange goods and explain what they would do with them. Ask the children to group the goods into different categories (e.g., food, clothing, toiletries, etc.). Ask the children to group the goods according to who would use them (mother, father, etc.). Ask them where the good came from and who might have brought it into the house and why.
Materials	Anything useful children wish to bring to class. *Note:* Teachers may want to bring their own articles to class instead of having the children bring things.

4 Wild Animal

8 Goods and Services

Objectives	Understanding the importance of food for good nutrition; getting to know that food is scarce and is a very important good; becoming familiar with animals that live in the wild.
Activity	Have a child pretend to be a wild animal in the jungle. Ask the child how it feels to be free. Make animal noises and have the class join in. Tell the wild animal that it has been without food all day. Ask the class, "Where will the wild animal find food?"
Getting Started	Play with the children by asking them to name different wild animals. Show the class pictures of many animals that live in the wild. Ask the class to make the noises that go with each animal. For a tiger say "Grrrrr," or for a wolf say "Ruffff." Have the children make wild animal faces on paper plates, which can be worn as masks. On other paper plates have them draw animal food such as nuts and insects. Children should be allowed to wear their masks and find food.
Follow-up Discussion	Where did the food come from? What would happen if a wild animal did not eat? Why is it important for wild animals to eat? What are some of the many kinds of food animals can eat? Where do our families get food? Who makes our food? Why is food a very important good? How can this good also be a "goodie"?
Materials	Paper plates. Stapler. String. Scissors. Crayons. Animal pictures. Marking pens. Construction paper.

5 Circle Game

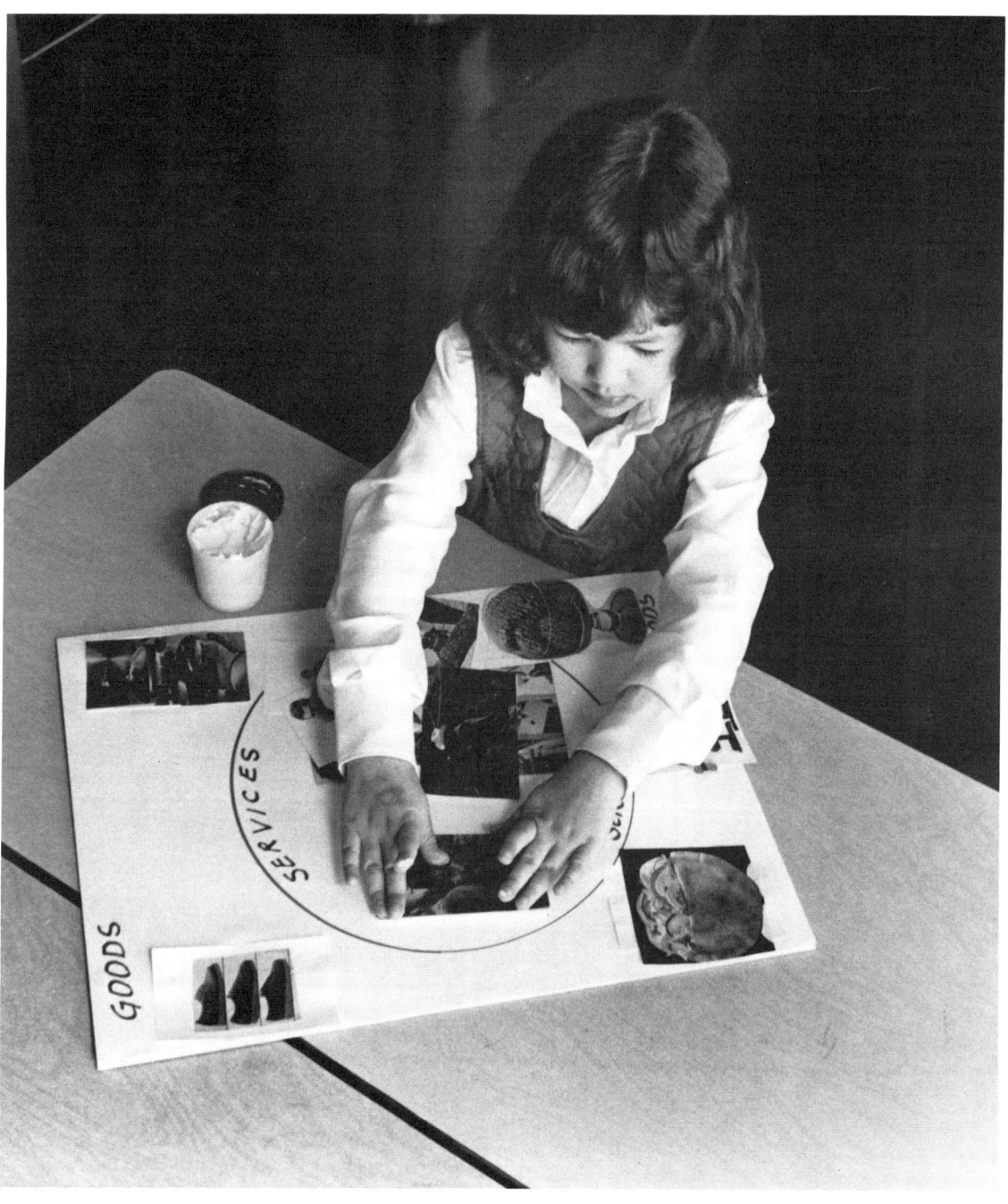

Objectives	Learning the difference between a good and a service.
Activity	Draw a circle on a large posterboard. Have children paste pictures of services inside the circle and those that are not services outside the circle.
Getting Started	Cut out of old magazines pictures such as of a teacher, a child playing, a football, ice cream, a child smiling, a barber cutting hair, a firefighter, a bus driver, a person delivering milk, a child swimming, etc. Give a child these pictures pasted onto 3" × 5" cards. Tell the child, "Paste the cards with pictures of services people do as *work* inside the circle. Paste the others outside the circle." You may want to let children each have a set of cards and a drawing of a circle to do this exercise at a work station.
Follow-up Discussion	Tell me a story about each of the pictures you pasted inside the circle. Why is each a service? Would you like to perform any of these services? What service would you like to do? Have you ever used the service in the picture? Does your mother perform any services? Does your father perform any services?
Materials	Posterboard. Marking pen. 3" × 5" cards. Paper paste. Old magazines. Scissors.

6 Hats and Shoes

12 Goods and Services

Objectives	Understanding the difference between a service performed by the government and a service performed by a business; understanding that government services are what almost everyone needs (but are not usually paid for when we get them) and are provided by officials of the community and that we pay businesses directly for their services.
Activity	Have children bring to class hats and shoes used for specific services by the people who perform those services. Have each child show her or his item to the class. Lead the class into a discussion of the services that go with each item.
Getting Started	Children should bring in hard hats, truckers' caps, professional baseball caps, firefighters' hats, sailors' hats, work boots, fishing boots, nurses' caps, etc. Pass out construction paper and have the children draw pictures of the persons who would use the items they brought. Have the children with items that would be used by government workers put a G on their papers and the ones who have items used by persons in business put a B on their papers.
Follow-up Discussion	What service does your person do? What person in your home does that service? Should you pay for that service when you get it? Who pays for that service? Does the person get paid by you for the service if that person gives it to you? Explain why governments provide services usually paid for by all members of a community whether they use them or not. Explain that businesses are paid directly for their services.
Materials	Hats. Shoes. Paper. Crayons or pens and pencils. *Note:* Teachers may wish to bring their own items to class.

7 The Raft, Part I (Shelter)

Objectives	Learning the difference between a necessity and other goods; learning some map skills and the relative sizes of the earth's land and ocean masses.
Activity	Read the following story. (*Note:* Fill in the appropriate blanks with the name of a harbor, students' names, and your name after M.) "Our class has boarded a large steamship at _____ harbor bound for the ocean island of Hawaii, our fiftieth state. (Show class the Hawaiian islands on the map.) After two days at sea a huge storm begins to rock our boat. _____ and _____ begin to scream, 'M _____, what are we going to do?' Just as we catch our breath to look out on the ship's deck, a giant wave picks us up like a large hand and sweeps us into the sea. As we look back up at the ship, a large rubber raft comes falling down on us. _____ reaches for it while _____ and _____ help everyone into it. We are so busy getting in that we forget to watch where the ship has gone—we are lost! 'LOOK,' cries _____. 'I see land!' 'Start paddling with your hands,' says M _____. 'It will be dark soon and we may lose our way.' Splashing and splashing and splashing, the class pushes the raft toward land. As the day grows darker and nighttime begins, we all wonder what we should do on this tiny uninhabited island we have found in the middle of the sea." The story is used as a basis for the class to understand what goods are necessities. In particular the class will learn the importance of shelter.
Getting Started	After the story is told, the teacher might ask the class, "It is going to be cold during the night on the island. What are we going to do? If we look around, maybe we will find a cave, some wood, or a big tree to sleep under." Direct the class into a discussion of what is probably found on a tropical island. Have the class tell you why they will first need shelter and why it is very important.
Follow-up Discussion	Why didn't we worry about getting toys on the island? Why was finding a place to sleep so important? Where do you sleep now? Is it safe and warm? Where did your family find it? Why is it so important? Did you ever think what it would be like not to have any shelter? Why is shelter a necessity or a good that is very needed?
Materials	Map of the world or a globe. Picture of an island.

8 The Raft, Part 2 (Food and Water)

16 Goods and Services

Objectives	Learning the difference between a necessity and other goods; learning different varieties of food in the four food groups.
Activity	The story of the class shipwrecked on a tropical island is continued from the first lesson entitled "The Raft." That lesson ended with the class discovering shelter as a necessity and as a primary good. In this lesson the class discusses why they now must begin their search for food. The four basic food groups—cereal, dairy products, meats, and vegetables—are introduced as the class talks about how they would search for them on this island. The class can discuss that meats are needed for building up the body to feel strong. Dairy products are good for bones and teeth. Fruits and vegetables provide needed vitamins and minerals for every part of the body to keep it working. Cereals give us energy.
Getting Started	The teacher might begin, "Now that we have a safe, warm place to sleep—WOW, am I hungry! Where will we find food? Where can we find clean fresh water?" The children should be told that there are fish in the sea to provide meat, grasses with seeds that provide grains, and vegetables and fruits growing everywhere. Animals will be needed to get dairy products, because milk and butter come from the milk of a cow, sheep, or goat. Lead the class into a discussion of how all this food will be found and what they will do with the food after it is found.
Follow-up Discussion	Why is food a necessity and not an ordinary good? Why is food, like shelter, something we need to stay alive? Why must all four basic food groups and water be found? Why must we eat all the different things on our plates at home and school? When can food seem more important than anything?
Materials	Picture of a tropical island. Map of the world or a globe.

9 The Raft, Part 3 (Clothing)

18   Goods and Services

Objectives	Learning the difference between a necessity and other goods.
Activity	The story of the class shipwrecked on a tropical island is continued from the two previous lessons entitled "The Raft." This lesson will add clothing as a primary good along with food and shelter, which was previously discussed. The story continues, "After we are happily fed and warm in our shelter, we have time to play. _____ and _____ begin a tugging game. Ooooops—he lost his shirt. _____ pulled it too hard. As we all look at his shirt we begin to wonder what we are going to do when all our clothes become worn out. That night it becomes very cold and windy and some of us have lost some of our clothes. What important necessity do we now need?" (*Note:* Put names of your students in the blanks.)
Getting Started	The teacher might ask, "Where does clothing come from?" The class might begin looking at each other's clothes, touching them and discovering that thousands of tiny threads are woven together to make cloth. Lead the class in a discussion of how they would begin a scavenger hunt around the island to find strands of plants to weave into cloth so the children can be protected from the weather.
Follow-up Discussion	What kinds of things may be found on the island to use as threads for making cloth? Why is clothing a necessity and not an ordinary good? Why is clothing, like food and shelter, something we need to stay alive? The most important goods are the goods that _____. After we have found all the necessities we need, what else might the class begin to do? Will we ever get home again to _____? Where does our clothing come from? Why don't we make all our own clothing? Why did each of you wear what you did today? What are the uses of different pieces of clothing you see around the classroom?
Materials	Clothing. Picture of an island. Map of the world or a globe.

10 Will It Last?

Objectives	Learning that goods that last for a long time are *durable* goods; learning that goods to be consumed almost right away are *nondurable* goods; learning that the value of a good depends in part on how long benefits from its use can be gained; using numbers one through ten and the colors red, blue, green, and yellow.
Activity	One work station should be set up in each of the four corners of the room. Each work station will have five durable and five nondurable goods. Each good will be labeled with numbers from one to ten. Each work station will be labeled with a color: red, blue, green, or yellow. Children will be sent one at a time to stations where they will find pieces of paper and four crayons (red, blue, green, and yellow). At each station the children will write the color of the station with the appropriate crayon on the top of their papers. The numbers of items that are durable goods should be listed in the left column, and the numbers of the nondurable items should be listed in the right column. Children should visit all four stations by waiting their turn and should turn in four complete reports.
Getting Started	What lasts longer: a lightbulb or a box of raisins? What kinds of goods do you own that last a long time? Name some important things that are consumed right away: a sandwich, an orange drink, a paper cup, etc. The teacher might say, "At each of the four stations set up around the classroom each of you are to get a piece of paper and write the name of the color shown at that station on the top. Then you are to write the numbers of all those items you think will last a long time—call them *durables*—at the left and the numbers of those items that are used right away—call them *nondurables*—on the right. Take your turn at each station and hand in to me four complete reports." (You may want to have the children circle the numbers of those items they have at home to discuss later.)
Follow-up Discussion	Why are both durable and nondurable goods very important items? Why are colors and numbers used to divide up the items?
Materials	Red, yellow, blue, and green crayons (four each). Four desks and chairs to make work stations. Red, yellow, blue, and green colored paper to mark work stations. Marking pen to write the color of the station on the appropriate paper. Four sheets of paper for each child. Forty tags to number goods. Pencils. Twenty durables (pen, stapler, box, etc.) and twenty nondurables (paper, box of raisins, tissue, etc).

11 I Wish I May, I Wish I Might!

Objectives	Understanding goods and services that are bought and sold as well as those goods and services that are provided "free" by nature; learning that we often want goods and services that exist only in our imagination.
Activity	Each child is given a sheet of 8½" × 11" white paper and crayons. Children are instructed to fold their paper in half. Then, with the fold facing them, they are to fold the paper in half again from left to right, making four sections out of the paper. Unfold paper. Children are to draw four wishes in the four sections.
Getting Started	The teacher might say, "Have you ever had a wish? Did you ever hope really hard for a trip to the mountains or a new bicycle? Today we are going to play the Wishing Game." Give children time to draw their wishes, and visit with the children individually so they can explain their drawings. Indicate which are goods or services that are bought and sold by businesses and which might be provided 'free' by nature. Those that are imaginary wishes can also be explained. Select several children who have a good variety of economic goods and services, free goods and services, and imaginary goods and services to show and tell the rest of the class. *Note:* Be sure not to discourage the childrens' imagination; imaginary goods and services can be very important to a child's happiness.
Follow-up Discussion	It's fun to wish for imaginary things, but why don't we find those things in stores? Why might some goods and services be called *economic goods* or *economic services*? Why might some goods and services be called *free goods* or *free services*? Can you think of some things we get for free? Why are the ocean, the sky, and the air free? Why are trips for vacations economic services? Who might help you and your family take a vacation?
Materials	White paper, 8½" × 11". Crayons.

12 This Is What I Want

24   Goods and Services

Objectives	Learning the difference between a consumer and a producer of goods and services; learning that each and every item or activity we want is produced, and that even though all are consumers, all are also producers; learning how to spell new words.
Activity	Each child is given a pencil and an 8½" × 11" white paper. The children are instructed to draw a picture of anything (a good or service) they would like to have. Children who are able should write at the bottom of the paper what they have drawn; others can do this with the help of the teacher. After the drawings are collected, pick several to discuss with the class where and how the pictured goods and services could be produced. Group students to decide which picture to discuss.
Getting Started	The teacher might say, "Did you ever wonder how a pencil is made or how one becomes a pencil maker? For every thing we want there must be someone who makes it. The makers, or creators, are the producers, and the users are the consumers." Discuss how everyone is a consumer and a producer: at home, in school, at work, and sometimes at play. Start the exercise.
Follow-up Discussion	You may want to repeat the exercise again with children drawing pictures of themselves producing goods or services. Why might a producer know what to produce? How do we choose what to buy, eat, use, or play with? How are you a producer? How are you a consumer? Is there some kind of producer you hope to be someday? Is there some kind of consumer you hope to be someday? Discuss with the class what goods and services are consumed in the classroom.
Materials	White paper, 8½" × 11". Pencils.

13 The Best Choice

26　Goods and Services

Objectives	Learning that everyone finds different value in a good or a service, because as individual consumers we choose what has the most value for us; understanding the central economic concept of scarcity of goods and services in every society.
Activity	A work station is set up in front of the room. Five numbered standing cards read 1, 2, 3, 4, and 5. On the work station table are five pictures of goods and services (e.g., ski trip, rubber duck, new boots, crayons, movie theater). Each child is given an opportunity to place a number in front of those items reflecting the order of her or his personal wants. The children are then given an opportunity to explain why they chose as they did.
Getting Started	The teacher might say, "Did you ever wonder why all things are not the same? Did you ever wonder why someone likes one thing but you like something else? As consumers, each of us has to choose—and choose wisely, as most of the time not enough of everything is made for everybody." Start the exercise.
Follow-up Discussion	How does your family choose? Why is choosing so hard? Why do your parents worry about choosing? Why can't we have everything we want? Did you ever see your mother or father choose in a store? What did they use to help them decide?
Materials	Cardboard. Marking pen. Old magazines.

14 Sports Station

Objectives	Identifying the wide variety of goods needed to play sports; understanding that sports are a very important entertainment service; developing prereading and spelling skills.
Activity	Set up four sports stations in the classroom. At each station place a clean trash can with a cover. Inside each can put ten to twelve items used to play a wide variety of sports (e.g., helmet, ski mask, baseball, etc.). Tag each item with its name clearly spelled out. A poster at each sports station should have magazine pictures of all the sports and their names spelled out next to them. A pile of 4" × 6" index cards should be placed at each sports station as well as one pencil. By turns, children go to each sports station. They pick one item from the can, copy its name and the name of the sport on a card, and proceed to the next station. All cards are turned in at the end of the exercise with the child's name on them.
Getting Started	The teacher might say, "Let's find out what we will need to play a sport. If you are a skier you will need a mask, gloves, skis, and poles. If you are a baseball player you will need a glove and of course a good ball." Each student takes a turn at a sports station, picks out an item from the can, and copies its name on the card on the sports station desk. Students should also copy the name of the sport from the poster next to the name of the sporting good. Each student can have a chance to go to all four stations and should turn in all four cards with his or her name on them at the end of the exercise. Start the exercise.
Follow-up Discussion	One by one, give students a chance to try to read the name of the sport and the sporting good and to explain why they go together. Talk to the class about why sporting events provide many jobs for people who make and sell sporting goods and who play and work at the events. Explain why entertainment from sports is healthy and a very important community service.
Materials	Sports magazines. Glue. Marking pen. Tape. Four posters. 4" × 6" index cards. Four clean trash cans with covers. Pencils.

15 Baseball Jobs

Objectives	Understanding the tools that are needed by producers of goods and services; learning about competition; identifying tools needed in service industries that may differ from industries that produce goods.
Activity	Draw on the chalkboard a baseball diamond. Draw first, second, and third base and home plate. Divide the class into two groups: Teams A and B. The teacher should begin by telling the class that the first team at bat will be determined by a flip of a coin. Heads will be Team A, and tails will be Team B. When at bat each player will get a base hit by guessing correctly a tool that a producer (whom the teacher will name) uses. Mark movements by the players with chalk marks on the board. Any team that has three players who at bat incorrectly name a tool will turn over the game to the other team. Each team gets ten times at bat. The winning team is the one that scores the most runs, as in a baseball game.
Getting Started	The teacher might say, "Let's play baseball jobs! The class will divide into two teams." Tell the first player of the first team at bat to name a tool a carpenter uses. The second player names another tool; the third player another tool; and so on until three players incorrectly name a tool a carpenter uses. Then the second team will have a chance, and so on. The teacher can get the teams started by describing the different things that, for example, a carpenter, a plumber, a furniture maker, homemaker, teacher, doctor, or a hairdresser might do.
Follow-up Discussion	Play the game in the same manner, but use only goods jobs. Play the game in the same manner, but use only service jobs. Play the game the same way, but this time have the players name the job when you name the tool.
Materials	Chalkboard. Chalk. Eraser.

Goods and Services

16 Listen and Do

Objectives	Understanding what goods and services are; identifying those goods and services we sing about in popular songs.
Activity	Have the class sing the following popular songs or any others recently sung in class. After each song, have the class identify those goods and services mentioned. 1. "Jingle Bells" (good) 2. "Take Me Out to the Ball Game" (service) 3. "You Are My Sunshine" (free service) 4. "I'm a Little Teapot" (good) 5. "You're a Grand Old Flag" (good)
Getting Started	The teacher might say, "We think *so* much about goods and services that we sing about them. Like 'Jingle Bells'—what a wonderful song we sing in the wintertime—and it's really about a good: bells!" Have the class sing a favorite song. Explain why songs are about goods and services we can buy but many are also about goods and services we get from nature or free from each other, like friendship.
Follow-up Discussion	After a song is finished, discuss where the goods or services in the song came from and how they were made. Have the class discuss things that they like and songs that tell stories about them.
Materials	Song sheets.

17 Spelling Blocks

34 Goods and Services

Objectives	Learning how to write words and match them to pictures; understanding the differences between a good and a service.
Activity	On the chalkboard tape pictures of the following five goods (pencil, bottle, puzzle, rocker, and cherry) and five services (repair, defend, police, clean, and sing). Number these 1 through 10, and write out the names of the goods and services under the pictures. Divide the class into ten groups of one or more children. Give each group ten 3″ × 5″ index cards and a wooden block. (Blocks have six sides numbered 1 through 6 and a letter on each side. Each block will be used to spell out one of the aforementioned goods or services. For instance, pencil: side 1—P, side 2—E, side 3—N, side 4—C, side 5—I, side 6—L). When a group gets its block the children should spell out the word on it on a card. Next to that word the group should spell out or mark the number of the picture on the chalkboard that corresponds to the word. After this is done the group should pass its block to the next group. Each group should use up all ten cards by having a chance to see all ten blocks.
Getting Started	"I'm going to have you divide up into ten groups. Each group can have one of these blocks and ten cards. Take your blocks and see that each side has a number and a letter or just a number. Write on your cards the letter on side 1, then next to it the letter on side 2, then next to it the letter on side 3, and so on until you have written out the whole word. "Now look at the chalkboard. Find what you have written and write the number of it on your card." Have the class pass the blocks clockwise to another group about every five minutes. Each time a new card is filled out until all ten are completed. Have students in the group write their names on the backs of each of the cards and turn them in.
Follow-up Discussion	Discuss with the class the training, skills, and things needed to perform each service or make each good. Explain how words are the symbols we use to discuss everything around us. If the students cannot read or count, you should go from group to group and help them.
Materials	Ten 1″ wooden blocks.　　Magazines. Cardboard.　　　　　　Pencil for each child. Marking pen.　　　　　　Ten times the class size in 3″ × 5″ index cards. Tape. Chalk.

18 Shopping in the Newspaper

Objectives	Understanding that producers and sellers of goods and services tell people about them in newspapers; understanding that we can comparison shop at home with a newspaper; learning math skills (addition).
Activity	Give each student a section of a Sunday newspaper and a pair of scissors. Tell each to cut out ads of toys, TVs, and record players. Have the class first pass in the TV ads, and tell them what the advertisements say. If they are second or third graders, have them take turns reading the different prices and places TVs are for sale. Do the same with the toys and record players.
Getting Started	The teacher might say, "Let's go shopping in a newspaper. You know how your mother or father find things they want in the newspaper. Today we are going to find where we can get a new toy, a TV, and a record player." Start the exercise.
Follow-up Discussion	What do you look for in an advertisement? How can advertisements save us time and money? Why should you check many places and see for yourself which is the best buy? Can you think of other places where goods and services are advertised? Math skills could be learned by adding up the cost of all three items the class chooses. Have individual groups add up the three items, and have the groups compare how much they might need to spend.
Materials	Two Sunday papers. Scissors for each student. Pencils. Papers.

19 Spelling Soccer

Objectives	Spelling simple words and describing goods and services; learning about competition and teamwork.
Activity	Divide the class into two groups. Draw at each end of the chalkboard a goal box. Mark twenty dashes for letters between the two goals. Pick the team to begin by flipping a coin—heads Team A, tails Team B. By turn have each member of a team spell out a good or service you name, and mark the letters in the dashes. Teams must tell you if the word they spelled is a good or a service before they get another word to spell. Filling in all the spaces scores a goal. If a student makes a mistake or if a team scores a goal, the turn goes to the other team. That team will erase all letters and try to fill the dashes to reach the goal. The first team to score ten goals wins the game.
Getting Started	The teacher might say, "Come on and play 'Spelling Soccer.' This half of the class is Team A, and the other half of the class is Team B. If I flip a head, Team A goes first; if it's a tail, Team B goes first. O.K., Team _____, spell *cup*. Is that a good or a service? Spell *apple*. Is that a good or a service? Spell *hunt*. Is that a good or a service?"
Follow-up Discussion	Discuss the training and skills needed for producing the various goods and services mentioned in the game.
Materials	Chalk. Chalkboard. Eraser.

20 Can of Peas

Objectives	Judging the value of a good by its size, quality, usefulness, and price.
Activity	Instruct each child to bring to class a can of green peas that has a price on it. Have each child stand and describe the size of the can (ounces by volume or weight), the name brand (that the children may have heard or seen before), the usefulness of peas to them (e.g., peas are a vegetable that helps bodies stay healthy), and the marked price (if shown by a price sticker, or stamped in ink). After the children have shared their information, collect all the cans and arrange them on a table—first group them according to size of the can, and then (within that group) by individual price.
Getting Started	The teacher might say, "Today we learn about peas. They are good for us because they are green vegetables, which help make our bodies strong. Each of you will have a chance to share with the class how much your can of peas weighs before it is opened (the weight is recorded on the label), and the brand name printed on the label that tells what company processed and packed the peas in the can. Find the price on the can—the price sticker or stamped price will tell you how much the can of peas cost. You will tell us if you have eaten peas like the ones in your can, and whether you liked them. Try to think why peas are useful." Start the exercise.
Follow-up Discussion	Do the same exercise with any other relatively inexpensive and *safe* household item.
Materials	Cans of peas.

SECTION TWO
SPECIALIZATION AND JOBS

lesson	main theme	page
1 Airplanes	Specialization	44
2 Jobs and Tools	Job tools	46
3 Police Officer, Baker, Firefighter, Farmer, and Teacher	Machines in jobs and careers	48
4 Help Wanted: Circus*	Job application and training	50
5 Let's Go Fishing	Fishing industry	52
6 What My Mom and Dad Do	How parents earn a living	54
7 Bread Line	Specialization for quality and speed	56
8 Library	Library jobs	58
9 Whispers	Jobs we depend on for goods and services	60
10 Charades	Skills and training for careers	62
11 The Crayon Box	Division of labor produces more	64
12 Jobs Help Us*	Jobs help us and the community	66
13 Occupation Rummy*	Goods and services from occupations	68
14 Paperweights*	Nature of the manufacturing process	70
15 Help Wanted	Job application and interview skills	72
16 Which Job Is Best for Me?*	Matching jobs with interests and ability	74
17 Building a Home*	Specialization in building jobs	76
18 Public Service Jobs (Government)	Jobs and services from government	78
19 Labor Unions*	Nature and purpose of labor unions	80
20 Classified Ads	Finding jobs in the newspaper	82

*For students who are readers and can write simple sentences.

Airplanes

44 Specialization and Jobs

Objectives	Getting to know that people working as a team, specializing in what they do best, can produce more and can produce more efficiently; learning that specialization leads to a higher standard of living for society.
Activity	Divide the class into two equal groups. Give each group one scissors, one roll of tape, and forty to fifty sheets of paper. Divide the chalkboard into two sections with a chalk line. The class teams are to produce airplanes and tape them onto their side of the chalkboard. The team that has taped the most completed airplanes to the chalkboard wins.
Airplane assembly instructions: Each sheet of 8½" × 11" paper must be folded in half and cut into pieces 4¼" × 5½". Each of these must be folded in half and opened. Fold two corners to make a point at the top of the paper. Refold along the original fold. Bend the wings out on each side.
Show the children how to make the airplanes and tape them to the chalkboard. Teachers will quickly see that the team that has organized itself so that it assigns specialized jobs will make the most airplanes. One team will be better at assigning one person to tape, one to cut, and others to fold the airplanes.
Getting Started	The teacher might say, "Everyone on this side of the classroom is Team A and everyone on this side of the classroom is Team B. I will show you how to cut a sheet of paper in half and make a paper airplane. Watch this!" After giving each team only one roll of tape, one scissors, and paper, tell each group they have fifteen minutes to get as many airplanes on their side of the chalkboard as they can.
Follow-up Discussion	Why did one of the teams produce more airplanes?
Why is making airplanes in a team just like people making many other kinds of things?
What other things could we make in teams?
Explain why jobs are specialized in a factory.
Who knows someone who works in a factory?
Which job did you think was the most fun?
Why can we make more things when we work together?
Materials	100 sheets of 8½" × 11" paper.
Two scissors.
Two rolls of tape.
Chalk.
Chalkboard.

2 Jobs and Tools

Objectives Understanding that jobs are specialized and require many special tools; relating specific tools to specific types of jobs; understanding the importance of tools in many careers; distinguishing among various shapes and objects; learning hand-eye coordination.

Activity Work stations are set up around the classroom. Each work station has a picture of someone doing a special job. On a poster laid out in front of each child are tracings of several tools needed to do that job. Children match the tools in front of them at their work stations with the drawings in front of them. Give children turns at visiting each work station.

Getting Started	Set up each work station with a picture of someone doing a special job (e.g. nurse, carpenter, gardener, construction worker, farmer, plumber, mechanic, postal worker, office worker). Place in a pile in front of that picture those tools that go with the special job and a poster with the tracings of each of the tools. The teacher might say, "Go to your work stations and you will find a picture of a hard-working person. All those things in front of you are tools the worker needs to do his or her job. Place these tools on the drawing of them on the poster." Have children exchange work stations and proceed in the same way again. If tools are too big to trace on the posterboard, then use masking tape and trace them out on the floor beside the work station.
Follow-up Discussion	Teachers can go around to each work station and explain what each tool is and what it does. After each child has done all the work stations, give children an opportunity to ask questions about the jobs and tools. Do you know someone who has this job? Where have you seen this tool before? Would you like to have this job? Why are tools so important to special jobs? Why do people have to know a great deal about their jobs? Can anyone do any job just as well? Why should people have their own special jobs?

Materials	Posterboard.
	Magazine pictures of workers doing their jobs.
	Marking pen.
	Paste.
	Masking tape.
	Tools:
	    Carpenter—screwdriver, pliers, ruler, level, drill.
	    Nurse—plastic thermometer, stethoscope, ear light, tongue depressor.
	    Plumber—wrench, hammer, pipe cutter.
	    Office worker—pen, stapler, date book, calendar, scissors.
	    Gardener—rake, shovel, snippers, sprayer.
	    Mechanic—socket wrench, screwdriver, sockets, wire cutters.
	    Postal worker—tape, scale, pen, stamp moistener.
	    Farmer—rake, hoe, shovel, shears, clippers.
	    Construction worker—trowel, hammer, putty knife, tin snips, etc.

3 Police Officer, Baker, Firefighter, Farmer, and Teacher

Objectives	Understanding that jobs are specialized and require many special tools and special machines.
Activity	Tape to the chalkboard the following pictures: police officer, baker, firefighter, farmer, and teacher. Provide each child with a piece of 8½" × 11" paper, crayons, scissors, and a ruler. Show the children how to divide their paper into eight sections. (Fold the paper in half, turn it to its side and fold it in half again and then in half again. When opened the paper will be divided into eight sections.) Instruct the children to draw the following eight items in the eight sections of their paper: whistle, ax, hoe, grade book, oven, projector, tractor, fire engine. Have the children cut out their drawings, put their names on the back of each picture they draw and tape them on the chalkboard below the jobs they belong with.
Getting Started	The teacher might say, "Today we are going to learn about *special* tools and *special* machines we use to do jobs that are *specialized*. People, tools, and machines work together to make us goods and provide us with services." The teacher may add, "Now you know why there is specialization!" Before you begin the exercise you may want to joke about how a police officer doesn't need an oven and a postal worker doesn't need a fire engine.
Follow-up Discussion	Repeat the exercise but with more sophisticated jobs, tools, and machines (e.g., computer programmer and a computer, stockbroker and a desk). As you check the children's drawings taped to the board, discuss how the tool or machine is used on the job. Ask the class what careers they may one day be interested in and why. If possible have the real people who do these jobs come into the classroom and discuss their jobs. In your school, you may find a nurse, a secretary, and a custodian who could explain their jobs, tools, and machines.
Materials	8½" × 11" paper. Crayons. Pictures of a police officer, baker, firefighter, farmer, and teacher. Tape. Scissors. Rulers.

4 Help Wanted: Circus

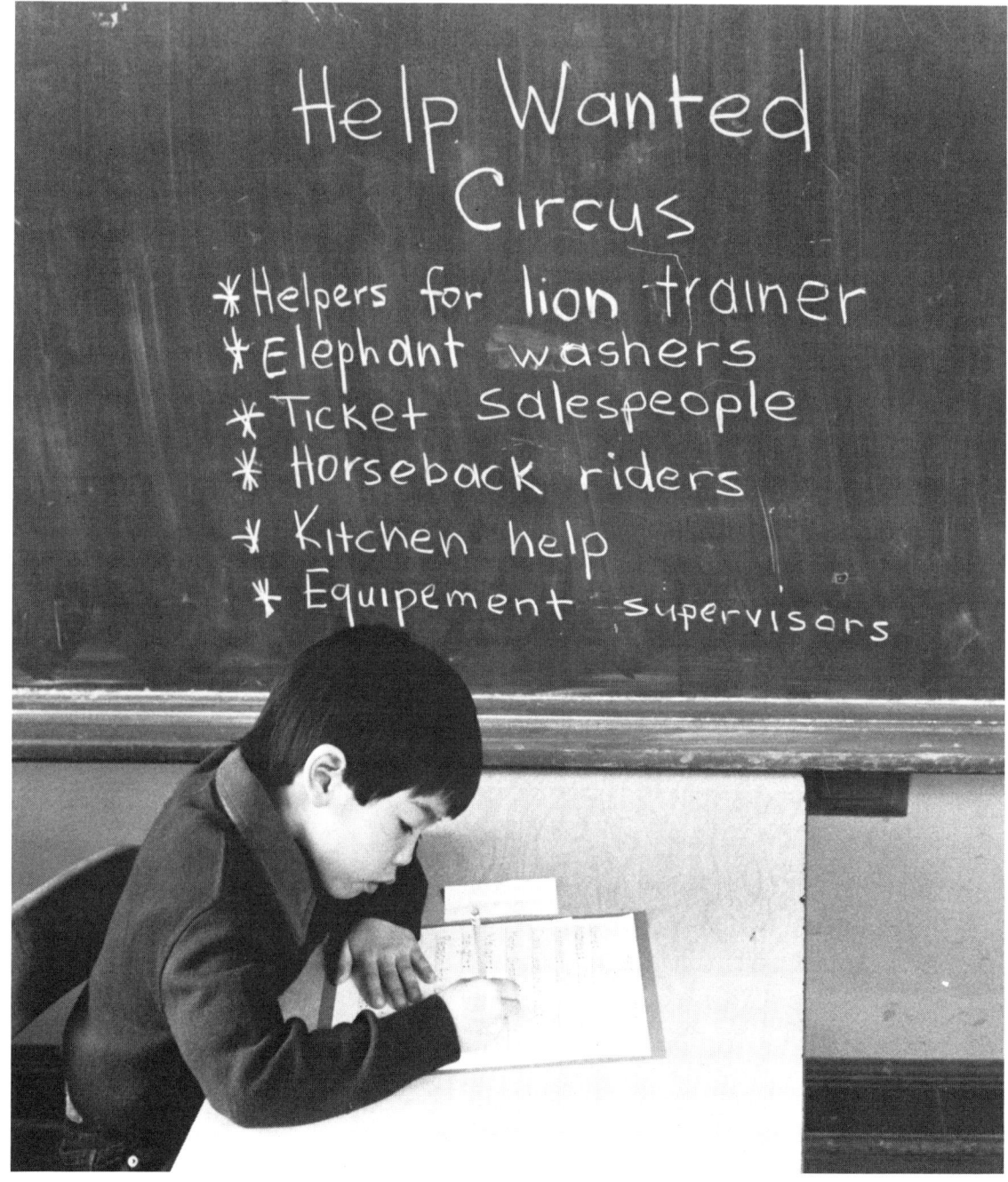

Specialization and Jobs

Objectives	Understanding the many specialized jobs needed in service industries; filling out a job application; understanding that people are selected for specific jobs because they have the skills and training needed for those jobs.
Activity	Prepare a simple job application form to be duplicated that asks: job applying for, name, address, telephone number, years of schooling, grades in math this year, grades in English or reading this year, weight, height, reason for applying, names of two references, and special skills or training. Pass out to each child a pencil, a job application, and some scratch paper. Write the following on the chalkboard: *HELP WANTED: CIRCUS, Helpers for lion trainer, elephant washers, ticket salespeople, horseback riders, kitchen help, and equipment supervisors.* Explain each of the jobs. Students will apply for any job they like by filling out the job application and passing it in to you. The teacher can hold interviews of candidates while the class watches.
Getting Started	The teacher might say, "Now we are going to find out how one gets a job. Jobs are very special, and each of you may already have special skills and training. How about working in a circus? Read the chalkboard with me." Start the exercise.
Follow-up Discussion	Complete the same exercise with a hotel or any other work area in which children will be able to help. Show the class the help wanted section of a newspaper and show them how to use it. Pass out sections of a Sunday newspaper's help-wanted section and have students find jobs for nurses, cooks, bookkeepers, etc. Read and discuss jobs they find.
Materials	Chalk. Chalkboard. Copier. 8½" × 11" paper. Pencils.

Specialization and Jobs

5 Let's Go Fishing

Objectives Understanding the specialization of job skills in industry; learning about jobs in the fishing industry; learning that fish is an important source of protein in a balanced diet; understanding that in industry many people work together to produce a certain good such as fish.

Activity Instruct each child the day before to bring in a lunch the next day that includes one item made with fish (e.g. a tuna, sardine or salmon salad sandwich). Hang up around the classroom pictures of fishing boats, fish, nets, and other things used in the fishing industry. Tell the class a story about the people involved in the fishing industry. Tell the children how the fishers' work made it possible for the class to have fish for lunch today. As an aside, reinforce the fact that fish is an important source of protein and one of the four food groups. Remember that the four food groups were taught as part of Lesson 8 in Section One.

Getting Started	"Suppose you were going to go into the fishing business. You would need a fishing boat or trawler, nets, a crew, and lots of supplies. On your boat you would need lunch for yourself and the crew and lots of ice to keep the fish fresh until you get back to port. You would also need rope, lots of hooks, and some bait. It would take many special jobs to get you ready. Imagine all the people who worked to make your boat: the lumberjack who cut down the trees; the truckers who brought the wood to the boat yard; the boat maker who must get the wood and some glass, nails, glue, and dozens of other things to put the boat together. Don't forget the people at the dock who would put your boat in the water. A lot of storekeepers would have to work to get your supplies. Net makers would make nets. Maybe you would be the captain of the boat. You would have to hire a crew to help you pull in the fish. Who would make the ice?—the ice maker. After you caught all the fish, people would have to help you unload. Some of your fish might go to a factory where fish like tuna is cooked and put into a can. Many people work there. Someone would have to pack all these cans into cases and ship them to stores. Remember many people will have to work in the store to price the cans of fish and clean the shelves. Someone will even put the can in a bag when you buy it. Maybe the sandwich you brought in today was made from that can of fish. As you can see, many people work together. The fishers, the factory workers, the crew on the dock, the grocer, and many others work together in special ways. Each specializes in a job." Give each child a chance to say which job he or she would like to do. After the story is over and the discussion finished, let the class have their lunch in the classroom for a change. Give plenty of opportunity for each child to talk about the story of fish.
Follow-up Discussion	What did each of you bring for lunch? Can you think of one of the jobs needed to make that lunch? Do the same type of exercise again, but base it on each child bringing in a lunch made with dairy products. Do the same exercise again, but, base it on peanuts, fruit, or even bread. You may want to set aside four days so you can deal with all four food groups—cereals, dairy products, meats, and vegetables.
Materials	Pictures of fish and fishing boats, nets, hooks, and other fishing supplies. Tape. Lunch made with fish for each child.

Specialization and Jobs   53

6 What My Mom and Dad Do

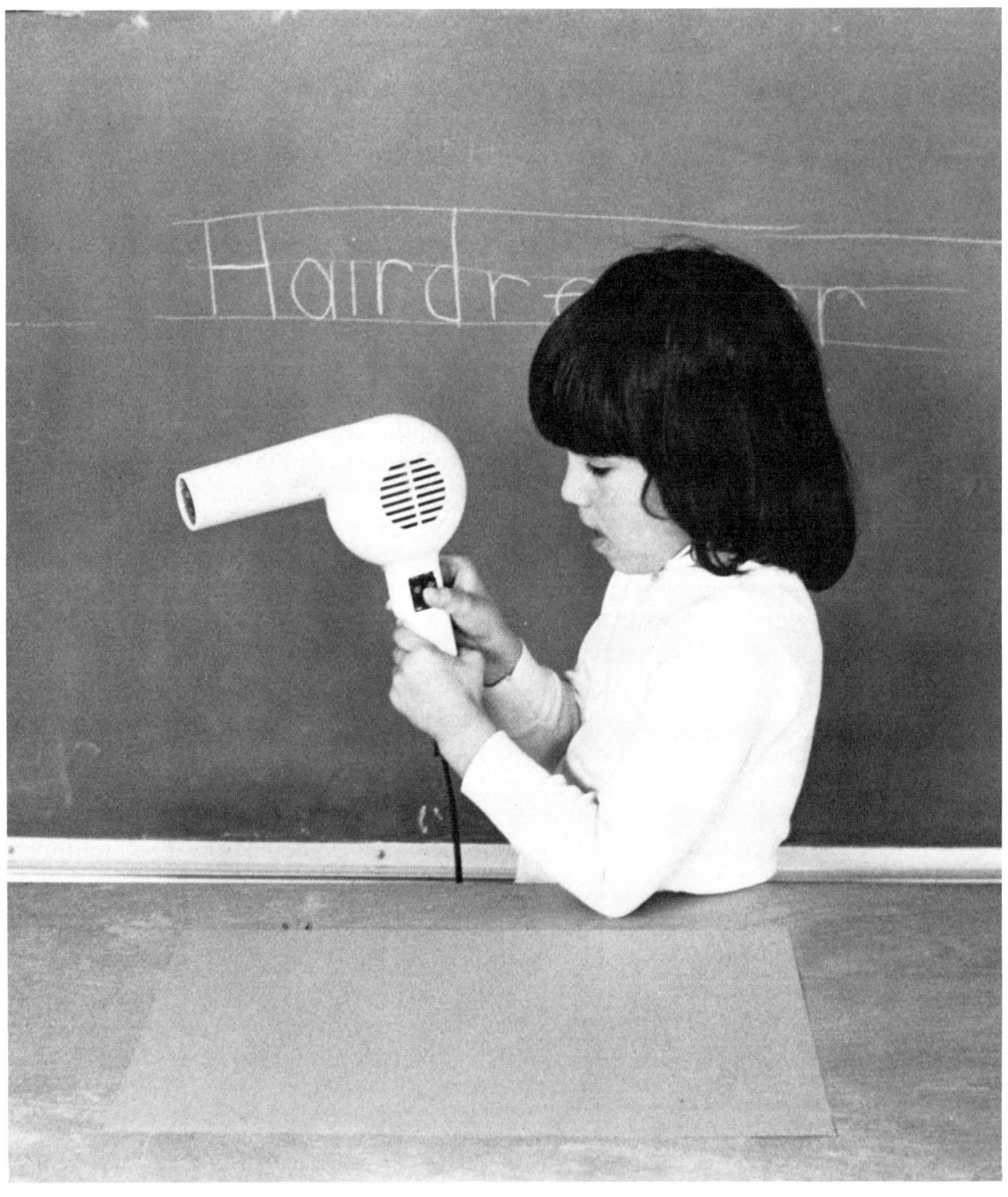

54   Specialization and Jobs

Objectives	Learning that each and every job is important in our economy; understanding that jobs are sometimes difficult and many times very interesting; learning about the jobs their parents have and how they make a living.
Activity	A day or two ahead of time, have the children interview their parents—whether they work inside or outside the home. Have them ask their parents the following questions: What time do you start work? What time do you finish work? What good or service do you provide? What other jobs are involved with your job? How did you first get interested in your job? Can others do what you do? Have the children bring in something each of their parents uses at work in the home or outside the home. One at a time, give the children an opportunity to report on what they found out about their parents.
Getting Started	The teacher might say, "Put on your desk what you have brought to class. Tell me why they are needed for the jobs your parents do. Tell the class the answers to the questions you brought home." You may need more than one class period if you have more than twenty students.
Follow-up Discussion	Have five of the children set up work stations around the room with what they have brought to class. Let the rest of the class visit these stations in an orderly way to learn about jobs. Rotate the work stations so each child has a chance to have one.
Materials	Items each child's parents use on the job.

7 Bread Line

56 Specialization and Jobs

Objectives	Understanding that a system of job specialization can increase the speed and quality of making goods.
Activity	Set up a long table with the following items in order: slices of bread, three toasters, paper plates, three butter knives, three open jars of jelly, paper cups, and two gallons of milk. Show the class how a glass of milk is poured and how toast with jelly is prepared. Allow fifteen minutes for the class as a whole to to prepare the milk and toast. Stop them when the time is up, and discuss with the class why very few children were able to get their food. Now do the exercise again. This time assign individual children to the tasks; e.g. assign two children to the slices of bread, three to the toasters, two to the paper plates, three to the butter knives, three to the jelly jars, and two to the gallons of milk. Have three children stand at the end of the table to set aside finished sets of glasses of milk with plates of jellied toast. Start the production line going and allow fifteen minutes for the exercise. Discuss with the class why this time it went much faster even though fewer children were working to prepare the food.
Getting Started	After the food is set up the teacher might say, "Watch how I make toast with jelly on a plate with a glass of milk. Now, all of you come up here and do the same." Clean up and set up again. "Why didn't all of you get yours?" Then say, "Now let us try it again, but this time we will do it like a production line." *Note:* Take safety precautions in using toasters and extension cord.
Follow-up Discussion	Where else are production lines used? Why is group production of goods faster than when each produces his or her own? Can you think of any other way we can use a production line in class?
Materials	Long table. Two slices of bread for each child. Three toasters. Extension cord. Two paper plates for each child. Three butter knives. Three jars of jelly. Two paper cups for each child. Two gallons of milk.

8 Library

58 Specialization and Jobs

Objectives	Understanding that many specialized jobs are done in a library; learning how a library is used; learning the importance of a library to a school and a community.
Activity	Bring the class to the school or community library. Before you leave have each student prepare one question about either jobs in the library or how the library is used. Arrange to have the librarian and assistant librarians discuss what they do, how they were trained, and how the library is used. Have the library custodian, secretary, and other library staff members explain their jobs. Give each child a chance to ask a question.
Getting Started	The teacher might say, "Today we are going to the school (or community) library. We will learn about all the important jobs in the library. You will learn how someone trains to work there. You will learn how you can use the library. Libraries are places where anyone can go to find answers to most questions. Each of you should bring one question you can ask the librarians about their job or about how to use the library." Start the exercise.
Follow-up Discussion	Why are people's jobs in the library specialized? How can you use the library? What is a question you would like to find the answer to? Would you like to work in a library? How does someone learn how to work in a library? How are some of the jobs in the library similar to jobs elsewhere?
Materials	Paper. Pencils.

9 Whispers

60 Specialization and Jobs

Objectives	Learning that almost everyone has a job; understanding that everyone's job helps someone else and that we depend upon many people for the goods and services we get.
Activity	Arrange the class in a circle around the outer walls of the classroom. Go up to the first child and whisper, "The farmer grows the grain, the factory worker makes it into cereal, the pilot eats the cereal so he can fly the farmer on vacation." Have the first child whisper this to the child on his or her left; then that child will whisper it to the next child and so on until the whisper is passed around the room and back to you. Have the last child who heard the whisper say it out loud to the class. Have the first child who heard the whisper say it out loud to the class. Discuss why the story changed and relate it to why we depend on each other a great deal in our economy.
Getting Started	The teacher might say, "We are going to play a game called 'Whispers.' Arrange yourselves in a circle around the walls of the room. I am going to whisper to _____ first, and then _____ will pass the whisper to the next child, and that child will pass it to the next child until the whisper is passed around the room to me again. Each of you should be very careful to let only the next child hear the whisper. The last child in the circle will repeat the whisper to the whole class." After the exercise is over write the whisper on the chalkboard for follow-up discussion.
Follow-up Discussion	Why did the story change? Why do we depend on each other? In what other ways do we depend on each other? How do we depend on each other in our jobs and in getting goods and services? How did the farmer help the factory worker? How did the factory worker help the pilot? How did the pilot help the farmer? How are our jobs and needs in the economy tied together like our circle? Why do things in the economy go wrong sometimes like they did in the circle?
Materials	Chalk. Chalkboard.

10 Charades

62 Specialization and Jobs

Objectives	Distinguishing among different careers; learning to act.
Activity	Tape on the chalkboard pictures of a police officer, a doctor, a teacher, a plumber, a carpenter, a pilot, a veterinarian, a jockey, a secretary, a dentist, a soldier, a lawyer, a taxi driver, a psychologist, an exterminator, and a mason. Pass out cards to sixteen students. Each is to get one card that has a picture of one of the professions on it. Select one child to play act silently her or his profession while the rest of the class looks at the chalkboard pictures to figure out what job is being acted out. Whoever guesses the profession correctly can act out her or his card until all are acted out. If one student guesses the professions twice or there are some students who guess the profession correctly and have no card, then the teacher should randomly select the next child. Children may use only paper, pencil, and a desk as props.
Getting Started	The teacher might say, "I am going to explain what each of the professions on the chalkboard are all about." After you are finished say, "Now let's play a game of charades. I will pass out cards with professions on them. On the chalkboard are all the same professions that are on the cards. While one of you tries to silently act out the profession on your card, the rest of the class will try to guess what it is." Start the exercise.
Follow-up Discussion	Who would like to be a plumber? Why? Who would like to be a pilot? Why? Who would like to be a police officer? Why? (Ask the same questions about all the professions that were acted out.) What professions are you interested in that I did not use? Tell the class about the skills and training needed for each profession discussed. Give the class time to draw out their own perceptions of one of the professions. Let them discuss their pictures later.
Materials	Pictures of a police officer, a doctor, a teacher, a plumber, a carpenter, a pilot, a veterinarian, a jockey, a secretary, a dentist, a soldier, a lawyer, a taxi driver, a psychologist, an exterminator, and a mason. Crayons. Paper. Sixteen 5" × 8" index cards. Marking pen. Chalk. Chalkboard.

11 The Crayon Box

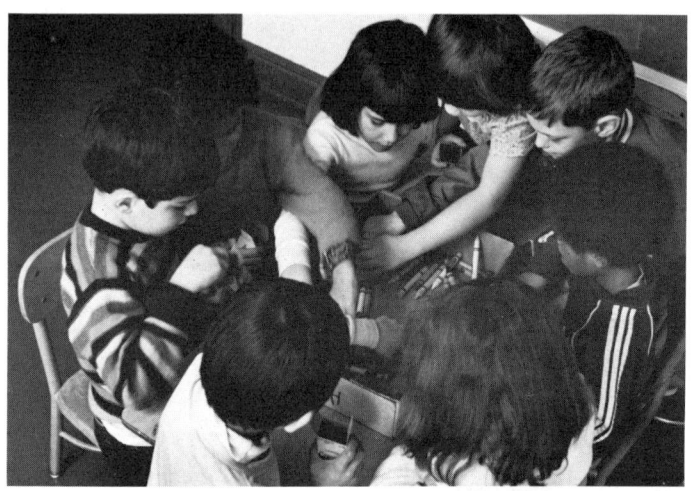

Objectives	Learning that specialization of jobs and the division of labor can make the production of goods more efficient; learning teamwork; learning colors.
Activity	Set up three tables with eight chairs at each table. Assign twenty-four students to the chairs. Put eight boxes of eight crayons each on each table. *Round 1:* Dump the crayons in a pile on each table. Time the groups as they

put all the crayons back into their boxes as they originally were. Discuss with each group how they went about the task. *Round 2:* Dump the crayons out again on each table. At each of the tables have each child collect one of the colors. Now the eight different colors will be piled up in front of the eight children at each table. Stack the empty boxes up at the end of each table. While you time them, have the children pass the empty box around; each child packs his or her own colored crayon into the box. Let them continue with each of the boxes until they are filled as they originally were. Discuss with each group how they went about the task.

Getting Started	The teacher might say, "I have set up three tables and will assign eight children to each table. You will find a pile of crayons on your table and a pile of empty crayon boxes. When I say *go* repack the boxes with eight different crayons in each. I will time each group to see which can do it the fastest. We will try this again later with each child putting in each box only one of the colors, like in a production line at a factory." Start the exercise. *Note:* If you have fewer than twenty-four children in your class, set up fewer tables. If you have more than twenty-four children use the extras as timers.
Follow-up Discussion	During the first round, what were some of your problems? Why did some of the groups in round 1 work faster than others? Why did all the groups work faster in round 2? How did the group divide up their jobs in round 2? Why was it easier to get organized in round 2? Where else is labor divided up? What tasks are done at school and at home like this? Why did we need eight workers at each table? You may want to reward the fastest group in each round. Repeat round 2 several times to improve efficiency.
Materials	Twenty-four boxes of crayons that have eight different colors in each. Three tables. Twenty-four chairs. At least one stopwatch.

Specialization and Jobs   **65**

12 Jobs Help Us

Objectives	Learning that different jobs help individuals and the community at large; learning the services provided by various professions.
Activity	In a column, write the following words on the chalkboard: *farmer, nurse, teacher, principal, firefighter, librarian, police officer, pilot, truck driver, grocer, dentist, postal worker, construction worker.* Then explain to the class what each profession involves. Beside this first column, write out the following sentences: *(1) People who help us get our food. (2) People who help us stay healthy. (3) People who help us learn. (4) People who help us stay safe. (5) People who help us move things.* At their seats, children should mark down a column of numbers 1 through 5 on a piece of paper. Next to each number they should write out the corresponding jobs.
Getting Started	The teacher might say, "How dangerous it would be if our homes caught fire! Who in the community could help us? That's right, firefighters. Like firefighters, there are many people who have jobs that help us. Today we are going to learn about some of these people. I can probably guess that some of you have already had many of the people whose jobs are on the chalkboard help you." Start the exercise.
Follow-up Discussion	Who else can help us get food? Who else can help us stay healthy? Who else can help us stay safe? Who else can help us learn? Who else can help us move our things where we want them to go?
Materials	Chalkboard. Chalk. Paper. Pencils.

13 Occupation Rummy

Specialization and Jobs

Objectives	Learning about many and varied occupations and the goods and services they provide.
Activity	Prepare four sets of cards. Each set should have twenty-four cards: twelve each with a picture of an occupation with that occupation spelled out and twelve each with the goods or services the occupations provide. (For example, one of the first twelve cards would read *farmer* and have a picture of a farmer. A corresponding card from the second group of twelve cards would have the word *corn*.) Each set of cards should have different occupations and corresponding goods and services. Divide the class into four groups. Give each group about fifteen minutes with each set of cards and have them match the occupations with the goods and services they provide.
Getting Started	The teacher might say, "I am going to divide the class into four groups. Each group has a set of cards. Before you look at your cards, I am going to tell you all about a great number of occupations. After I finish, match each of the occupation cards with the good or service card showing what each can produce or make." Go around to each group and give help as needed. Encourage each group to finish in about fifteen minutes so all four sets of cards can be seen by each group in an hour. Be sure to shuffle the cards before groups exchange sets.
Follow-up Discussion	If time is a problem, you can prepare four identical sets so all four groups can work simultaneously. Another variation is to make separate sets of just service occupations and separate sets of just goods occupations with their corresponding good or service cards.
Materials	Ninety-six 4" × 6" index cards. Marking pen. Old magazines. Glue or tape.

14 Paperweights

Objectives   Understanding the nature of a manufacturing process; understanding how workers cooperate in mass production; learning to divide labor into specific, specialized tasks; taking pride in the accomplishment of making a quality product.

Activity	A group of work stations are set up into a production line. Work station 1: two children near a sink to wash off small rocks (one inch in diameter). Work station 2: two children nearby at a desk with towels to dry the rocks. Work station 3: two children seated at a desk with blowdryers to completely dry the rocks. Work station 4: two children seated at a desk covered with newspapers to paint the rocks with a fast-drying latex paint. Work station 5: two children seated at a desk covered with newspapers to blow dry the painted rocks. Work station 6: two children seated at a desk covered with newspapers to glue the painted rocks to two-inch plywood squares. Three remaining students can line up the finished paperweights on an empty desk. Remaining children in the class can stand by as quality control observers. Produce enough paperweights for the entire class. Extras could be made as a class fundraiser. Explain to the class why their activity is very similar to a manufacturing process.
Getting Started	The teacher might say, "We are going to set up a paperweight factory in our classroom today. Each of you will have a job either producing paperweights or as a quality control observer. The quality control observers will make sure every paperweight is made perfectly. We want to be proud of what we make." Direct the class to begin the manufacturing of paperweights. Make sure to use the suggestions from the observers to improve the quality of the product.
Follow-up Discussion	What were some of the problems with our production process? What other things can you guess are made with a production process? Why did we divide up the jobs in the production process? How could we produce more and better paperweights? How could you do your job better? Have students set up two competing teams to see which group can make the better quality paperweight in a certain amount of time. What are some of the drawbacks of a production line job?
Materials	Five old towels. One small rock, one inch in diameter, for each child. Four blow dryers. Two extension cords. Two cans of quick-drying latex paint. Two paintbrushes. Two tubes of quick-drying glue. One two-inch square piece of plywood for each child.

Specialization and Jobs

15 Help Wanted

Objectives	Understanding how people specialize in the production of services; matching abilities with a job market; learning how to interview for a job; learning how to fill out a job application.
Activity	Write at the top of a large poster *HELP WANTED*. Below that write, "Students needed for general classroom work." List the following jobs: book shelf manager, lunchbox coordinator, homework collector, calendar monitor, exercise chairperson, line leader, trash collector, sink cleaner, cleanliness inspector, chalkboard cleaner, desk and chair organizer, and light and heat manager. Leave space below each job to fill in names of students. Feel free to add other jobs as needed. Explain to the class what each job involves. Leave a space on the poster to list students who are unemployed. Pass out applications for jobs that include: name; years of education; experience; special skills; reason for applying; and first, second, and third job choices. Interview students and pick the best-qualified students for each job. Engage students in their jobs as long as class time will allow.
Getting Started	The teacher might say, "The class is going to learn how to get a job! On this poster is a large help-wanted advertisement. Each of you will have an opportunity to apply for a job." Start the exercise.
Follow-up Discussion	Leave time at the end of the day for students to discuss their jobs. Rotate jobs every few days so students can learn about different jobs. Why is it difficult to be unemployed when others are working? Why does the classroom run more efficiently by dividing up class jobs? Monitor students to coach them into doing a better job. Reward better workers with a longer recess or a special table where they can talk as much as they want in the lunchroom.
Materials	Large poster. Marking pen. Tape.

16 Which Job Is Best for Me?

Objectives Learning about one's own interests and abilities; learning about jobs that relate to specific interests and abilities; identifying what type of job one would like to do.

Activity Prepare a checklist to be passed out to the class. Students check one answer to each of the following questions on the checklist: (1) I like to work _____ alone, _____ with one other person, _____ with many people. (2) I like to work _____ outside, _____ inside. (3) I enjoy more _____ working with my hands, _____ working with my thoughts. (4) When working _____ I like to talk, _____ I like to be quiet. (5) I would rather _____ work the same hours each day, _____ work different hours each day.

(6) I would like to _____ make things, _____ show other people how to make things. (7) When working _____ I would like to do things quickly, _____ I would like to make fewer things slowly. (8) I would rather _____ sell goods or services, _____ make goods or perform services.

As children look at their answers, explain how the checklist could help them decide what job might be best for them. For example, for question 1 explain that radio announcers, researchers, and custodians usually work alone; storekeepers, doctors, and attorneys sometimes work with one other person; and actors and teachers work with many other people. Catalog on the chalkboard the numbers of children that made each choice. Explain that the class has many and varied interests that can fit the many and varied jobs in our economy.*

Getting Started	The teacher may say, "Did you ever wonder why so many people have so many different jobs? Each and every one of us has different abilities and interests. We are very lucky that we do, because we need so many different goods and services every day. What kinds of goods and services did you use today? I am going to pass out a checklist to help you find your own interests in a job." Start the exercise.
Follow-up Discussion	Which of the jobs mentioned fits your interests and abilities? Why must we begin to plan early to train for many of these jobs? Why did many of us have different interests? Why are differences good for our economy? How did we explain why people work in so many and varied jobs? Why is each and every job an important job?
Materials	Paper. Pencils. Typewriter. Copier.

*Note: The *Occupational Outlook Handbook* prepared by the U.S. Department of Labor may help you gather information on other occupations.

17 Building a Home

Objectives	Understanding that many specialized skills and materials are needed in producing goods; associating a job with the kinds of materials used in that job; learning the importance of division of labor in building a home.
Activity	Display a dollhouse in front of the class. Divide the chalkboard into four columns.

Label column 1 *What is needed*, column 2 *Type of job*, column 3 *Tools*, and column 4 *Materials*. Make the following lists under each column:

What is needed	Tools	Type of job	Materials
clearing the land	hammer	bulldozer	wood
pouring a concrete foundation	screwdriver	operator	nails
	cement mixer	mason	shingles
framing the wooden structure	truck	carpenter	wire
	bulldozer	plumber	electric tape
putting in pipes and a water system	pipe cutter	electrician	electric switches
	wire cutter	heating and cooling contractor	air conditioner
wiring the home for electricity	shovel		heater
	hoe		pipes
putting in a heating and cooling system	shears	paving worker	electrical outlets
	saw	city road worker	putty
	paintbrush	landscape gardener	curb stones
putting up wallboards inside, and finishing all the woodwork	knife		tar
	paint roller		concrete
	tar roller		wallboard
	spade		paint
paving a driveway to the house	clippers		grass seed
			trees
putting in a street and curb in front of the house			water
			good soil
landscaping the house lot			

Discuss with the class what all of these things are. In groups of three, children should try to organize what is needed in column 1 with jobs, tools, and materials in the other columns. Visit with individual groups to help them in this task. After the exercise, arrange items from all columns under items that are needed. Relate jobs with tools, materials, and services in building a home.

Getting Started	The teacher might say, "Did you ever wonder what it takes to build a home? Look at this dollhouse. Imagine it is a real house in the country. It may even be a home being built for your family. Many, many workers are needed to build a home. They will need many, many materials and special tools and machines." Start the exercise.
Follow-up Discussion	Have you ever seen a home being built? Do you know anyone who has one of these jobs? As a class assignment, have children discuss with parents about the people who helped build their homes. Have them report to the class. Bring some of the tools and materials needed in the above jobs for further discussion.
Materials	Dollhouse. Paper. Chalk. Pencils. Chalkboard.

18 Public Service Jobs (Government)

Objectives Learning that the community provides many services through local, state, and the federal government; learning that these services are mainly paid for by taxes; understanding the training of government workers; appreciating the importance of the services public employees provide.

Activity Explain to the class that government services are provided locally by the town, statewide by the state government, and nationally by the federal government. Use your own town and state as an example. This can be done by drawing a large circle on the chalkboard labeled *U.S.A.*

78 Specialization and Jobs

Inside that circle draw a smaller circle labeled *your state,* and inside that circle draw an even smaller circle labeled *your town.* Next to these circles label three columns *Town, State,* and *Nation.* Complete the columns with lists as shown:

Town	State	Nation	
trash collection	tax collection	tax collection	Army
town engineer	health department	health department	Navy
dog pound	library	library	Marines
tax collection	justice department	justice department	police
health department	lawmakers	lawmakers	
library	recreation/parks	recreation/parks	
justice department	roads	Coast Guard	
lawmakers	public colleges and universities	Air Force	
recreation/parks		roads/highways	
roads	police	postal department	
public schools	social services	social services	
police	national guard	housing department	
social services	sanitation		
sanitation	public schools		

Explain to the class the nature of each of these services and the types of jobs in each area. Use the drawing with circles to explain how each level of government services overlaps other levels of services. Explain that many of these services are essential to the general health and welfare of our economy.

Getting Started

The teacher might say, "Today we will learn that part of the price of things we buy and part of the money workers make is saved as taxes to pay for very important services. Did you ever wonder who made the highway or paid for the police? When you go to the park or use the town library, someone is there to help you. These services and many others are provided by the government. We will learn about these services and about the workers who provide these services. We will also learn how they are paid for." Start the exercise.

Follow-up Discussion

Have students draw pictures of how they perceive one type of public service job.
Have students discuss their drawings.
Which services have you used?
Why are public services so important?
Do any of you know public servants?
Which job would you like to do?
Another class period could be used to discuss how each worker is trained.
Invite people to class to explain their public service jobs.

Materials

Paper.
Crayons.
Chalkboard.
Chalk.

Specialization and Jobs

19 Labor Unions

Objectives	Understanding how a labor union is formed; learning the functions labor unions perform; learning how management and labor unions collectively bargain.
Activity	Write on the chalkboard LABOR UNION. Explain that labor means workers and union means having one worker talk to the boss for all the workers. Below the words LABOR UNION write MANAGEMENT (*Teacher*) and LABOR (*students*). List the following jobs: *arranging chairs, erasing and cleaning chalkboard, cafeteria line leader, homework collector, attendance clerk, recess police, timekeeper, exercise leader, sink orderly, bus line leader, patrol leader, health inspector.* Pass out 3" × 5" index cards. Instruct students to nominate one child as their union leader by writing his/her name on a card. Tell students that they cannot elect themselves. Collect the cards and count the votes for the union leader, who should discuss job assignments and negotiate (with the teacher) who will be assigned the different jobs. When all the assignments are made, the class will vote on the union-negotiated agreement. Majority vote is needed. Students should do their jobs during the normal class day. If they have complaints about their jobs or would like other jobs, they must pass in green 3" × 5" index cards to the union leader with their complaints. All complaints or grievances are negotiated with management with green cards. The union leader should give workers the answers to their grievances.
Getting Started	The teacher might say, "We are going to learn about labor unions. Labor means workers and union means having one worker talk to the boss for all workers. Unions are a way for workers together to explain their problems to their bosses. Labor unions elect a spokesperson by voting. This spokesperson is called the union leader. He or she will try to get answers to worker problems by talking with the boss or management. All agreements the leader gets that influence all workers must be voted on by all the workers." Start the exercise.
Follow-up Discussion	Did you find the union leader helpful? Would you like to have a spokesperson ask your boss questions for you? Do you think we should elect different union leaders from time to time? Did you get the job you wanted?
Materials	White 3" × 5" index cards. Green 3" × 5" index cards. Chalkboard. Chalk.

20 Classified Ads

Objectives	Learning how to find jobs in the newspaper; learning about the types of jobs available locally; understanding the types of training and experience needed in finding a job.
Activity	Divide the class into five groups. Give each group a copy of a help-wanted section of a Sunday newspaper. Group 1 will circle all nursing jobs, group 2 all secretarial jobs, group 3 all sales jobs, group 4 all mechanic jobs, and group 5 all accounting jobs. Visit individually with each group to explain each kind of job. Give each group one marking pen.
Getting Started	The teacher may say, "Here is a section of a Sunday newspaper. Did you ever see one of these around the home? If we look into the newspaper we will find a section called 'Help Wanted.' In this section is a list of jobs. I am going to divide the class into five sections to search for jobs." Start the exercise.
Follow-up Discussion	Have groups count up the number of jobs in each category. Calculate the mean salary for each type of job and compare them. Explain the different types of information in each ad. Read a few ads out loud and explain them. Have you ever seen a classified ad before? Do you know of anyone finding a job this way? What are some important things to look for in an ad?
Materials	Five Sunday newspapers. Chalk. Chalkboard.

SECTION THREE
RESOURCES

lesson	main theme	page
1 Factors of Production	Land, labor, capital, and management	86
2 Salvage Game	Resources and goods	88
3 Resource Match	Resources in production	90
4 The Big Tree	Managing resources	92
5 The Vacant Lot	Government and business resources	94
6 Some Grow Back	Renewable and non-renewable resources	96
7 Farms and Factories	Land use	98
8 Our Town	Land resources	100
9 Animals	Animal resources	102
10 Labor	Labor resources	104
11 Capital	Capital resources—Money	106
12 Management*	Management resources	108
13 The Maze	Skilled, unskilled, and professional labor	110
14 American Indians' Resources	Capital resources-tools	112
15 The Globe	Maps and land resources	114
16 Resource Match	Resources in production	116
17 Building a House	Factors of production in building a house	118
18 Education	Human capital—Education	120
19 Stickers	Identifying resources	122
20 Family*	Resources and jobs	124

*For students who are readers and can write simple sentences.

Factors of Production

Objectives	Learning that the four factors of production in any production process are land, labor, capital, and the coordination of these called management; understanding that resources used to produce goods and services are called factors of production.
Activity	Give each child a file folder. Have the children place their names and the words *Resources are Factors of Production* on the folder covers. Pass out four sheets of white paper to each child. Have children write one of the following words at the top of each sheet of paper: *land, labor, capital,* and *management*. Describe to the class any production process. For example, you could describe the production of wheat. Tell the class about the farmer, who is the labor. Describe his land. Show the class pictures of the machinery and tools (or capital) that the farmer uses. Describe the managers of the large farms of today as businesspeople who coordinate the farm work. Have children draw pictures of the factors of production on their paper. You can repeat the exercise with other paper and other examples of a production process. Have children collect sets of factors of production in their folders. Give children the opportunity to discuss their work.
Getting Started	The teacher might say, "Think about what goes into making something. What do you need to make a baseball, a sandwich, an automobile, or a bottle of soda? We need lots of resources to make things. To grow wheat for bread, for example, we need some land—the farmland to grow our wheat. We need a farmer, maybe you! We need the tools or capital and someone with the mind to manage the entire business." Start the exercise.
Follow-up Discussion	Why are all four factors always needed? What would happen to production if one factor were lost? Why is some land better than other land? How can we find the best labor? How does education improve labor? How can new ideas make our capital work better? Why is it important for management to organize production?
Materials	File folders. White paper. Crayons. Stapler. Marking pens.

2 Salvage Game

88 Resources

Objectives	Learning about the basic resources that are used to make goods; becoming familiar with the fact that many varied goods are made from similar resources; learning about colors.
Activity	Each child is given a package of stickers. Each child's stickers should be a different color. Children will use their stickers to mark resources in the classroom. After the class has been told about wood coming from trees, a child should be sent to explore the room to mark with her or his stickers items that have wood in them. Other children will do the same with items made of glass, plastic, metal, and cloth. If the class is larger than five, several children can have the same assignment. After all the children are done, begin a discussion of the many items that now have stickers.
Getting Started	The teacher might ask, "What do you think is made from trees in the forest?" Lead the class in a discussion of what wood looks like. Show the class something made out of wood. The teacher might say, "How shiny metal is! Look at this bright metal stapler." You can also talk about what plastic, glass, and cloth look like. When you feel confident that each student knows the feel or texture of the resource and how it looks, send each child out in the classroom to salvage these resources by marking them with colored stickers.
Follow-up Discussion	The same activity can be done in a playground—wood, cloth, metal, plastic, and glass items can be identified by children with colored stickers. Can you see through glass? What happens to glass when you drop it? What are some colors of wood? How does a piece of wood feel? Is metal shiny? Do things made of metal feel smooth or rough? Is cloth hard or soft? Is cloth made in only one color? Are things made of plastic bright and shiny? Can you break plastic very easily? Look at this chair. Can you tell me all the resources in it?
Materials	Basic classroom items for children to identify for wood: Pencils, chairs, tables, paper. For glass: eyeglasses, drinking glasses, windows, dishes. For metal: pens, staplers, chairs, door frames. For cloth: shirts, trousers, curtains, and tablecloths. For plastic: drinking cups, ruler, comb. Five colors of peel-off stickers.

3 Resource Match

Objectives	Identifying the four factors of production: land, labor, capital, and management; understanding that the resources used to produce goods and services are called factors of production.
Activity	Cut red, blue, green, and yellow paper (8½" × 11") into quarters. Make enough so each child can have three of each color. Mark red pieces *LAND*, blue pieces *LABOR*, green pieces *CAPITAL*, and yellow pieces *MANAGEMENT*. Make twelve poster-size work stations around the room as follows. Each work station should have a poster with a picture of a resource and a pocket for colored cards behind it with a slot in the front for cards to be inserted. Make three work stations for each resource. Pass out the colored cards. Have children mark their names on their cards. In an orderly fashion, have children deposit their cards to match the posters. One resource match could be for raisins. The three land posters could show the lot of the factory, the grapes growing in a field, and the road in front of the factory. The three labor resources could be a production-line worker, an office worker, and a worker loading boxes onto a truck. The capital resources could be the delivery truck and the packing machines. The management resources could be a supervisor wearing a hard hat on the production-line floor, a person behind a desk, and a person going over records. After all the cards have been deposited, collect them and review with the children the ones that were placed incorrectly.
Getting Started	The teacher might say, "I will pass out to each of you twelve cards. These cards are red, blue, green, and yellow. Red is for land, blue is for labor, green is for capital, and yellow is for management. Put your name on each one. Around the room you can see work stations showing resources. Place each of your cards in a slot in a poster that shows the resource written on your card." Start the exercise.
Follow-up Discussion	You may wish to use the pictures children did in lesson 1 for the posters. Have children discuss the posters after they have finished. Discuss with the class how the factors are combined to produce things.
Materials	Posters. 8½" × 11" red, blue, yellow, and green paper. Marking pen. Magazines. Glue. Tape. Scissors.

4 The Big Tree

Objectives	Learning that resources are finite; understanding how precious our resources are and the need to effectively manage them.
Activity	Use pieces of brown and green paper to create a big tree in front of the classroom. Each piece of the tree should be attached with a small circle of tape so it can be easily removed and replaced. After the tree is constructed, tell children what kinds of things are made from wood. Ask the class what they might like to make from the tree. Each time a child makes a suggestion, remove one piece of the tree. Continue until most of the tree is removed. Tell the class what would happen if we used up all our trees. There would be no parks and we could not make any more wood products. Ask the class which items they think they could live without. Each time a suggestion is made, return one part of the tree. Continue until about three-quarters of the tree remains. Tell the class the importance of balancing our need for resources and preserving them.
Getting Started	The teacher might say, "Look at the big tree in front of the class. What could we make from the wood in the big tree? Can you guess?" Start the exercise.
Follow-up Discussion	Why is wood a natural resource? Why have we protected such large amounts of forest in our country? Why is it important to use resources to create jobs and products we need? Why should resources be managed carefully? Repeat the exercise later with a big oil well or a big fish.
Materials	Twenty sheets each of brown paper and green paper (8½" × 11"). Tape. Scissors.

5 The Vacant Lot

Objectives	Learning that choices must be made about how to use our resources; understanding that in our economy most resource decisions are made by individual businesses and individual consumers but that government can also decide how resources are to be used.
Activity	Take a picture and make a slide of a vacant lot in a downtown location. Project the slide in front of the class. Ask "What can this land be used for?" Give time for children to make several suggestions (e.g., a firehouse, a shopping center, a school, a church or temple). Ask "How will the decision be made on how to use the land?" Give time for children to answer. Explain why in our economy most decisions to use resources are made by business, such as in the case of a shopping center. Tell them also that the government may decide, as in the case of a firehouse or a school. Explain how in each case certain groups of citizens benefit. Stress how resources are used wisely by business when they provide what we need. Indicate how governments try to provide what consumers need. You may wish to show other slides of finished buildings nearby.
Getting Started	The teacher might say, "Did you ever walk by a building or a park and wonder who put it there? Did you wonder why it was there? How are decisions made to use our resources such as land? Let's find out." Start the exercise.
Follow-up Discussion	Show slides of public and private building projects in your town or city. If an actual building project is underway in your town, take slides of it during the various stages of construction. Use it as an actual example of how resources were used in your community. Explain how decisions are made to build buildings, and indicate what benefits they bring. Explain that not all decisions are accepted by everyone.
Materials	Camera. Slide film. Slide projector. Screen.

6 Some Grow Back

Objectives	Understanding the difference between renewable and nonrenewable natural resources; learning that both need to be managed wisely and that nonrenewable resources may never be replaced.
Activity	At the top of a sheet of paper write *Some Grow Back*. Divide the sheet into nine sections (three rows of three blocks). In the top three blocks write *coal, oil,* and *water*. In the middle three blocks write *trees, air,* and *rubber*. On the bottom three blocks write *beef, iron,* and *gas*. Duplicate this sheet for every child. Pass out the sheets to the children. Give each child five red chips to mark nonrenewable resources and five green chips to mark renewable resources. Explain what each resource is and have the children guess which chip to place over each word. Facilitate the exercise by walking around the room to see how each child is doing.
Getting Started	The teacher might say, "Some resources grow back. Some resources such as peas and corn can be planted and harvested year after year. These resources are called renewable resources. Other resources are more scarce. They are limited. It took centuries for oil to be formed, for example. The world has only so much oil. We don't know exactly how it was made so we can't make it exactly the same way. When the oil runs out it will be nonrenewable. I am going to pass out some playing boards of paper and some chips. As I describe a resource you are to place a chip on it. If you think it can grow back—renewable—place a green chip on it. If you think it cannot grow back—nonrenewable—place a red chip on it." Start the exercise.
Follow-up Discussion	Can you name other renewable resources? Can you name some other nonrenewable resources? How are some resources replaced? How can we replace some nonrenewable resources? What resources do you use? Are they renewable? Which three of the four factors of production are renewable? Do the same exercise with different resources on the playing boards. Play the same type of game, but play it like "Bingo."
Materials	8½" × 11" white paper. Red and green chips. Marking pen. Copier.

7 Farms and Factories

Objectives	Learning the various uses of the natural resource, land.
Activity	Divide the class into five groups. Give all the children crayons and paper. Have each of the five groups draw pictures of one of the following: roads, schools, homes, factories, and farms. Have each group explain what they have drawn. Lead the class in a discussion of how land can be used for each of the uses named.
Getting Started	The teacher might say, "What would you use land for? I will divide the class into five groups. Each will draw a picture of how they are to use their land. One will use theirs for roads, another for schools, and others for homes, factories, and farms." Start the exercise.
Follow-up Discussion	Which use was most important? Why are all uses of land very important? Do you have land? How do you use it? Why is land a factor of production? Can you think of any other uses of land? What can we take from the land? What items in the classroom came from land? Everything?
Materials	Crayons. Paper. *Note:* You may wish to have students collect all their resource lessons in the file folder made in Lesson 1.

8 Our Town

Objectives	Learning the various uses of land resources in your own community.
Activity	Obtain five maps of your town from a local real estate office. With a pen, divide each map into sections. Draw lines around residential areas, shopping areas, government-owned schools and buildings, business districts, farms, and manufacturing areas. Make a transparency of one of the maps. Divide the class into five groups. Give one map to each group. Make sure each group has a yellow crayon to color in residential areas, a green crayon to color shopping areas, an orange crayon to color government areas, a blue crayon to color business districts, a red crayon to color farms, and a purple crayon to color manufacturing areas. As you project your transparency before the class, indicate the various areas on the map and have children in the groups take turns coloring in their maps. Mark your own school on the map first. Help children find their own houses or apartments.
Getting Started	The teacher might say, "Have you seen your own home from the sky? Maps are drawings of places as they would look from the sky. Everything is smaller. This is a map of our town. Look! Here is our school." Start the exercise.
Follow-up Discussion	Do all towns divide their land like we do? Is there anything special about how land was used in our town? What used the most land in our town? What areas of land have not been used? What might be a good way to use vacant land? Why is land used to produce almost everything?
Materials	Overhead projector. Transparency. Crayons (red, blue, green, yellow, purple, and orange). Maps of your town. Marking pen.

9 Animals

Objectives	Understanding the uses of animals as natural resources; learning that animals are the source of many goods; identifying goods produced from animals.
Activity	Set up four work stations in the classroom. Display a picture of one of the following animals on each poster: cow, sheep, chicken, and pig. Write the name of the animal shown on each poster. Tape an envelope on each poster with the pocket facing out. Prepare at least thirty index cards with pictures of animal products. For example, for cows prepare a card with a picture of a carton of milk, one with a package of cheese, one with a leather jacket, and one with a hamburger. For sheep prepare a card with a picture of a wool sweater, one with a roasted leg of lamb, one with a wool cap, and one with a wool rug. For chickens prepare a card with a picture of a barbecued chicken, one with an omelette, and one with scrambled eggs. For pigs prepare a card with a picture of pigskin gloves, one with a roasted ham, and one with fried bacon. Have children one at a time pick up a card, show it to the class, and place it in the envelope pocket of the appropriate poster. Have the class watch as each child places his or her card. After the cards are all placed correctly, show the entire class the group of cards that go with each animal. Stress the importance of animals in our lives.
Getting Started	The teacher might say, "When you go to a farm, what types of animals do you see? Have you ever seen a pig, a cow, a sheep, or a chicken? Think about animals. They are resources too! Many of the goods we use every day come from animals. Animals are very important to all of us. We are going to learn why!" Start the exercise.
Follow-up Discussion	What are you wearing that came from an animal? Which animal did it come from? Can you name another important animal we get goods from? What do we get from goats? Why are animals resources? Are animals renewable or nonrenewable? Do any of you live on a farm? Tell us about it. Take the class to a farm after the exercise.
Materials	Old magazines. Scissors. Tape. Index cards. Marking pen.

10 Labor

104 Resources

Objectives	Learning that labor is a factor of production; understanding the differences among skilled, unskilled, and professional labor.
Activity	Divide the class into six groups. Explain what the differences are among a skilled, unskilled, and a professional laborer. Give to each child a sheet listing forty separate occupations. Have children in two of the groups circle skilled laborers. Have children in another two groups circle unskilled laborers. Have children in the remaining two groups circle professional laborers. Allow children in groups to work together. Have the children mark their names on their papers, and collect finished papers.
Getting Started	The teacher might say, "There are many jobs in our economy. Workers are labor. Labor is another one of our four factors of production. Labor is divided into three types. One is skilled. Skilled workers can do special jobs. Carpenters, for example, are skilled. They learn their craft or skill from working many years with an experienced carpenter. Unskilled workers work at jobs too. They do things that need little training. People who bag potatoes, fill our cars with gasoline, or clean our roads are unskilled workers. Professional workers have a great deal of education or a very special talent. Doctors, teachers, and lawyers must study for a long time to learn their jobs. Football players are professionals too! They have special talents." Begin the exercise by stressing that each job category is a unit of labor in some production process of a good or service and that each laborer is important.
Follow-up Discussion	Review exercises from Section Two on specialization and jobs. What type of laborer would you like to be? Why is labor the one resource we all hope to sell? Why do skilled, unskilled, and professional laborers work together? Why is training important for labor? Why do you go to school to learn job skills? Have children openly discuss the jobs they are interested in.
Materials	Copier. Typewriter. Marking pens.

11 Capital

Objectives	Learning that capital can be the money needed to buy resources to start a business; learning that money is a resource; learning that money is important in facilitating exchanges of goods and services.
Activity	Instruct the class that tomorrow you will serve lunch in the classroom. Question the class to be sure you serve something that everyone can eat. Tell the children that if they turn the class into a cafeteria tomorrow, then they will need four factors of production. The labor to prepare the food will be you and the children. The management to organize the meal will be you. The land and building will be the classroom. What is needed, tell the class, is the capital or money to buy the food. Because everyone will "buy" their food in class you will need some money now to buy the food. Explain that the capital (money to buy resources) must come from a loan. Pass out play money from which to borrow. Write down each creditor. Serve lunch the following day, collect lunch play money, and pay back your creditors. Explain to the class the importance of capital for every business to get started. Explain that interest is often paid to use someone else's money.
Getting Started	The teacher might ask, "If we were to turn this class into a cafeteria for tomorrow, what would we need? Who would be the labor? Who would be management, where would the land and building be, and where would we get the capital or money to buy the food?" Explain that you have everything but the capital. Start the exercise.
Follow-up Discussion	Why is money or capital a resource? Can we start businesses without capital? Where can we go to borrow capital? Explain what is needed to get a loan. Explain how businesses get loans. See Section Four, "Money and the Bank," for more on capital.
Materials	Materials to prepare lunch in the classroom. Play money (made from blackline masters in appendix).

12 Management

Objectives	Understanding that management is one of the factors of production; learning that management is a resource.
Activity	Divide the class into four groups. Group 1 are farmers. Group 2 are shoe manufacturers. Group 3 are grocery store owners. Group 4 are barbershop owners. Have each group answer the following question: What decisions need to be made? Have each group list the decisions. Assign one of the children in each group to be a discussion leader. The leader will write down the ideas and present the group's ideas to the class. Visit with each group to help them write out their ideas. Stress that the discussion leader is also a manager.
Getting Started	The teacher might say: "Each of you will be a manager today. I will divide the class into four groups. Group 1 are farmers. Group 2 are shoe manufacturers. Group 3 are grocery store owners. Group 4 are barbershop owners. I will pick one member of each group to be the leader. The leaders will list the decisions that need to be made to start their businesses." Start the exercise.
Follow-up Discussion	Why is management a factor of production? Why is organization important in making things? Can you name other managers? Is managing as important as providing land, capital, or labor? Is it difficult to be a manager? Why?
Materials	Paper. Pencils.

13 The Maze

Objectives Learning that labor resources are of different levels; learning that skilled, unskilled, and professional workers receive different wages; learning that training for an occupation can increase one's earning ability.

Activity Prepare four sets of index cards. Each set has eighteen cards. All sets have six cards with unskilled jobs, six cards with skilled jobs, and six cards with professional jobs. The unskilled jobs are: (1) raking leaves, (2) washing cars, (3) picking up litter, (4) collecting movie tickets, (5) picking oranges, and (6) mowing the lawn. The six skilled jobs are: (1) making a floor, (2) building a house, (3) building a parking lot, (4) cutting and styling

110 Resources

hair, (5) repairing a car, and (6) fixing a leaky water pipe. The six professional jobs are: (1) fixing a broken arm, (2) teaching a class, (3) making medicine, (4) running a bank, (5) defending a country, (6) making a court decision. Prepare four game boards. Each is an 8½" × 11" sheet of paper with a trail of thirty blocks drawn on it. The first of the blocks should read *Start* and the last of the blocks should read *Finish*. Prepare four spinning wheels five inches in diameter. Divide each wheel into four equal sections numbered 1, 2, 3, and 4. Color the spinners blue. Prepare four spinning boards, with yellow spinners, with the numbers 3, 4, 5, and 6. Prepare four spinning boards, with green spinners with the numbers 5, 6, 7, and 8. Divide the class into four groups. Give each group one set of cards and one of each color spinner. Give each child a marking chip to use on the playing board. Describe the eighteen jobs on the cards and explain the differences among professional, skilled, and unskilled labor. Have the groups shuffle their cards. Each child picks a card. If an unskilled job is picked, the blue spinner is used to find out how many spaces to move on the board. If a skilled job is picked, the yellow spinner is used. If a professional job is picked, the green spinner is used. Have each group play until one child passes the finish line.

Getting Started

The teacher might say, "Some jobs take more training than others. One can learn to wash a car very quickly. One can learn to pick up leaves very quickly too! It takes a longer time to learn how to build a house or to fix a car. Doctors and lawyers have to study a very long time to learn their jobs. Usually the harder it is to learn a job, the more money we get for doing that job. We are going to learn the differences among skilled, unskilled, and professional jobs." Start the exercise.

Follow-up Discussion

Why should the doctor move along faster than the car washer in our game?
Is it true that many times skilled workers are paid more than unskilled workers? Why? Is that fair?
Describe the training needed for the jobs in the game.
Explain why, as in the game, often some unskilled workers are paid the same or more than some skilled workers when their abilities are scarce. The same follows for professional and skilled workers.
Play the game again with other jobs.

Materials

Four 8½" × 11" pieces of white cardboard.
72 white index cards.
Marking pens (yellow, green, and blue).
Chips for markers.
Black pen.
Spinners and pins.
Ruler.

14 American Indians' Resources

Objectives	Learning that most labor is improved with tools; learning that tools and supplies are capital resources in the production process.
Activity	Instruct each child to prepare an American Indian project for class the next day. (This activity should be done in conjunction with a social studies unit on American Indians.) They are to research either the tools, supplies, or buildings used by Indians in the 18th century in the United States. The projects should include making models of buildings or making the tools or supplies used in the production of goods and services.
Getting Started	The teacher might say, "What did the American Indians do? They were very busy producing the goods and services they needed. Every meal involved many jobs. Every piece of clothing used a lot of labor. They used tools to do a faster and better job. They built shelter where they could work. Each of you will do a project on American Indians for class tomorrow." Start the exercise.
Follow-up Discussion	Give each child an opportunity to show and tell about her or his project. Explain to the class why tools are so important in the production of goods and services. Why did Native Americans use tools? Do we use today any of the tools American Indians used? Why are tools considered a factor of production? Which factor of production is tools? Which factor of production is shelter? How do capital resources improve labor resources? What other factors are needed in production? Can you name some of these factors American Indians used?
Materials	Children provide their own materials from home.

15 The Globe

Objectives	Locating various countries on a globe; improving map and globe skills; learning that land resources are located around the globe; learning the location of various precious productive resources.
Activity	Divide the class into four groups. Provide each group with a globe and stickers (green, yellow, blue, and white). Mark at the top of four columns on the chalkboard *green, yellow, blue,* and *white.* Under *green* write wheat: *Canada, U.S.A.,* and *Australia.* Under *yellow* write *oil: U.S.S.R., U.S.A.,* and *Saudi Arabia.* Under *blue* write *lumber: Brazil, U.S.A., Canada* and *Finland.* Under *white* write *rice: Thailand, Japan, U.S.A.,* and *China.* Have one child in each group take one color of stickers and mark the appropriate countries on the globe. Visit the groups to make sure all the stickers are placed correctly as shown on the chalkboard.
Getting Started	The teacher might say, "Look at this globe. It is a small model of our world. Look! Here is our town. It looks very small, but everything has been made small so the whole world can be shown. The things we need come from all over the world. We are going to locate the countries on the globe we get resources from. I have four globes, so I am going to divide you into four groups." Start the exercise.
Follow-up Discussion	Use different colored stickers and different resources. Combine this exercise with a geography lesson. Have students investigate other resources that come from the countries mentioned.
Materials	Four globes. Peel-off stickers (blue, yellow, green, and white). Chalk. Chalkboard.

16 Resource Match

116　Resources

Objectives	Learning that all four factors of production (land, labor, capital, and management) are needed in the production of all goods and services; learning that the marketplace is where factors of production are traded.
Activity	Prepare four times as many index cards as there are children in the class. One-quarter of the cards should read *labor*, one-quarter *land*, one-quarter *capital*, and one-quarter *management*. Shuffle the cards and randomly give four to each child. All at once allow children in the middle of the classroom floor to trade until each child gets one of each type of card. Explain that real factors of production need to be traded in a way very much like this to get all four factors of production.
Getting Started	The teacher might say, "All things we use were made with four factors of production. Land was needed for a place to make the product. Labor had to put it together. Capital, or tools or machines, were needed to help put it together. Managers were needed to see that all the jobs were done. We are going to play a card-trading game. You are going to trade to be sure you have all four factors of production." Start the exercise.
Follow-up Discussion	Do the same exercise, but prepare cards for one type of production. Use different sets for different productions, and repeat the exercise many times. Use industries in your town for examples. Ask children what factors exist in your town. Explain that many of the factors in your town were traded from far away. Explain the marketplace as an efficient place to find factors.
Materials	White index cards. Marking pen.

17 Building a House

Objectives	Learning the four basic factors of production: land, labor, capital, and management; applying the concept of factors of production to building a house.
Activity	Prepare four sets of four spinners. Prepare each set as follows: cut four circular pieces of cardboard five inches in diameter, and mark off one-quarter of the area of each spinner in a pie-slice shape; mark the slice on one of the spinners *land* and the other three *labor, capital,* and *management.* With a pin, attach an arrow to the middle of each spinner. Prepare four times as many cards as there are children in the class. One-quarter of the cards should read *labor,* one-quarter *capital,* one-quarter *land,* and one-quarter *management.* Divide the class into four groups. Provide each group with a set of spinners and a quarter of all the cards. Instruct children that they need four factors of production to build their homes. In each group let children take turns spinning the arrow on each of the four spinners. Each group should continue taking turns until one child landed at least once on the marked section of each spinner and collected at least one of each card. When each group has a winner, the four winners will compete orally by trying to explain how the four factors would be used to build a house.
Getting Started	The teacher might say, "We are each going to pretend we are building a house. In groups you will take turns using four spinners. Each in turn will try to get one capital card, one land card, one labor card, and one management card. The first four from the four groups to get all four cards will compete, and explain how the four factors would be used to build a house." Start the exercise.
Follow-up Discussion	Use the same spinners and cards but a different production of a good. Try the same exercise with a production of a service. Use the same exercise with a production in your town. Why are all four factors needed? Why does each spinner represent a separate factor market? Are any of the factors more important than another?
Materials	Pins. Cardboard. Crayons. Marking pen. Ruler. White index cards. Scissors.

18 Education

Objectives	Learning that education is very important to create or improve human capital; learning that education is an investment in oneself for the improvement of oneself for living and working.
Activity	Prepare four spinners as follows: Cut four circular pieces of cardboard ten inches in diameter. Divide each piece of pie-shaped cardboard into ten slices that are numbered 1 to 10, and place an arrow in the center of each circle with a pin. Divide the class into four groups and give each group a spinner. Give each child one turn to find out from the spinner how many years of training beyond high school she or he will get. On the chalkboard write the following careers with years of training needed: *physician*—10 years, professor—10 years, veterinarian—9 years, dentist—8 years, pharmacist—6 years, carpenter—5 years, plumber—5 years, engineer—4 years, accountant—4 years, dental assistant—3 years, licensed practical nurse—3 years, office manager—2 years, bookkeeper—2 years, retail store clerk—1 year, bank teller—1 year. Have the children pick professions from the list based on the years of training they have from turns on the spinners. Give each child an opportunity to tell whether she or he likes the choice she or he has made. Discuss with the class training as an investment in human capital.
Getting Started	The teacher might say, "Every job requires some training. On the chalkboard is a list of occupations and the number of years of training needed after high school. When you have your turn on the spinner, you will find out how many years of training you have. Each of you should pick a career from the list on the chalkboard. Later each of you will have a chance to discuss your choice." Start the exercise.
Follow-up Discussion	Repeat the exercise with different occupations. Try to choose occupations that fit the families of your children and the community they live in. Adjust the numbers on the spinners so different types of occupations can be done. Why is education a kind of capital resource? Why is education an investment? Do you think it is always a good idea to get as much training as possible? How many years of training do you think you will need? Why is it important to do well in school now?
Materials	Cardboard. Marking pens. Ruler. Pins. Chalk. Chalkboard.

19 Stickers

Objectives	Learning that many different resources are combined in the production of a good or service; understanding how to identify which resources are used in a good or service.
Activity	Write the following words on the chalkboard: *rubber, steel, glass, paint, leather,* and *plastic*. Explain to the class what each of these resources is. Explain where they come from and how they are produced. Display a bicycle in front of the class. Choose six children to come forward. Give each child a different color of stickers. Tell them that they are detectives. Have one child put his or her stickers where he or she finds rubber on the bicycle, and similarly the other children use their stickers to identify the other resources listed. After they have finished, have the children return to their seats. Review with the class the resources the children have identified on the bicycle.
Getting Started	The teacher might say, "I have written out six resources that are used in building a bicycle. Look at the bicycle over here. We use workers or labor in making bicycles. Can you think of how? We use capital in making bicycles. Can you think of how? We also need management in making bicycles. Can you think of how? Managers help organize the workers to use the things listed on the chalkboard. Workers make the bicycle." Explain how each resource is used. Start the exercise.
Follow-up Discussion	Could you build a bicycle without rubber? steel? glass? paint? leather? plastic? Where do the resources listed come from? Why is labor and management needed too? Do a lot of people work together to make one bicycle? Repeat the exercise with another product. Do the same exercise, but divide the class into groups, giving each group its own stickers and product.
Materials	Bicycle. Six colors of peel-off stickers. Chalk. Chalkboard.

20 Family

Objectives	Learning that everyone needs resources in his or her job; understanding that all people are themselves resources; learning the many and varied jobs of parents.
Activity	For a homework assignment, have children interview their parents. Have them ask the following questions: Do you work inside or outside the home? What do you like about your job? What do you dislike about your job? Is land needed in your job? Is labor needed in your job? Is management needed in your job? Is capital needed in your job? What resources do you use? Could you do your job without resources? Have students prepare a report from their answers for class the next day.
Getting Started	The teacher might say, "Resources are in everything we do. We use resources at school. We use resources at home. We even use resources when we play. I want each of you to find out what resources your parents need in their jobs. Ask your parents these questions and report to the class what you find." Start the exercise.
Follow-up Discussion	Can you name some labor resources? Can you name some capital resources? Can you name some land resources? Can you name some management resources? Why are each of the resources important? Could you make something if you had one resource missing? Why are we resources? Why are our parents resources? Why are we each producers? Why are we each a consumer?
Materials	Pencils. Paper.

SECTION FOUR
MONEY AND THE BANK

lesson	main theme	page
1 Big Nickel, Little Dime	Money as a unit of account	128
2 The One-dollar Bill	Recognizing a dollar bill	130
3 Bill-matching Game*	U.S. currency	132
4 Spending a Dollar	Spending and scarcity	134
5 Money Math	Math with money	136
6 Heads—You Win!	Coins and historical figures	138
7 Dogs	Barter	140
8 Barter/Trade	Barter and the marketplace	142
9 Vegetable Money	Basic math, buying, money as a medium of exchange	144
10 The Bank	Bank functions	146
11 Shopping Spree	Determination of prices	148
12 Money Math Is for Me!*	Basic math, buying, and selling	150
13 Checks	Checks	152
14 Green Card, Red Card*	Determination of price	154
15 Crayon Money	Money supply, prices, and inflation	156
16 Money Madness	Basic math, earning, savings, and spending	158
17 Make a Deal	Supply, demand, the marketplace, and equilibrium price	160
18 Why Prices?	Supply, demand, producers, and consumers	162
19 Around the World	Basic math, spending, saving, and earning	164
20 Jobs and Money	Wages and expenses	166

* For students who are readers and can write simple sentences.

Big Nickel, Little Dime

Objectives	Learning that money is a unit of account; understanding the size and shape of various coins and associating this with the coin's value; understanding how to count up to 100.
Activity	Set up work stations in the following way. Each child at a work station is given 1 dollar, 4 quarters, 20 nickels, 10 dimes, and 100 pennies. (Play money is used for this activity. Use the blackline master in the appendix for this lesson to make the play money.) The work station will have a poster showing enough circles and a rectangle to fit all the money. The poster will show graphically that one dollar equals four quarters equals ten dimes equals twenty nickels equals one hundred pennies. Explain what the coins and paper money are by visiting with individual work stations. Stress with children how to differentiate coins and bills by the size and pictures on each.
Getting Started	"Go to a work station. On the poster in front of you are circles and a rectangle. Place the coins on the circles they match. Place the dollar bill on the rectangle it matches." Explain to individual children why each group of coins is equal to each other group of coins and the dollar bill. Start the exercise.
Follow-up Discussion	Demonstrate what *actual* pennies, nickels, dimes, quarters and one-dollar bills look like. Which coin is worth the most? Can you think of any other coins? Let's count the pennies, nickels, dimes, and quarters! Why is there only one dollar bill? Are nickels bigger or smaller than dimes? Is a dime or a nickel worth more? Is a dime or a quarter worth more? Is a penny or a nickel worth more? What could you buy with a dollar? What could you buy with a quarter? Could you get a gumball for a penny? Whose pictures are on the penny, nickel, dime, quarter, and dollar? Repeat the exercise with half-dollars included.
Materials	Poster for each work station. Marking pen. Play money: 1 dollar bill, 4 quarters, 10 dimes, 20 nickels, and 100 pennies for each work station (use the blackline masters in the appendix to duplicate the play money).

2 The One-dollar Bill

130   Money and the Bank

Objectives   Learning to recognize all the markings on the one-dollar bill; understanding the story of money through markings on a dollar bill.

Activity   Distribute copies of a *diagram* of a one-dollar bill (made from the blackline master in the appendix). Explain that number *1* shows that dollars can be used to pay for goods and services, and it explains that people can exchange things for a dollar; *2* shows that the national bank that distributes these is the Federal Reserve (a dollar is one of their paper notes); *3* is the seal of one of the twelve branches of the Federal Reserve that gives out dollars; *4* is the seal of the U.S. Treasury, which uses its printing presses to make the dollars for the Federal Reserve Banks; *5* is the serial number of this dollar (each bill has a separate number); *6* is the metal-plate number that was used to print this dollar; *7* is the year this style of dollar was designed. From time to time the design of a dollar changes. Number *7* also shows that each dollar is signed by the secretary of the treasury. Have children look at their copies as you explain the numbers. Quiz the class on these seven points. Show them a real dollar and repeat the exercise.

Getting Started   The teacher might say, "The most popular bill used is the one-dollar bill. We are going to learn the seven points of a one-dollar bill. These points show everyone who earns or spends a dollar bill that it is a real dollar." Start the exercise.

Follow-up Discussion   Set up work stations where children identify the seven points on a dollar bill.
Show on a map of the U.S. the locations of the twelve Federal Reserve bank cities (Boston, New York, Philadelphia, Cleveland, Richmond, Atlanta, Chicago, St. Louis, Minneapolis, Kansas City, Dallas, and San Francisco).

Materials   Copier.
Paper.
Pencils.
Blackline master of enlarged one-dollar bill in the appendix.

3 Bill-matching Game

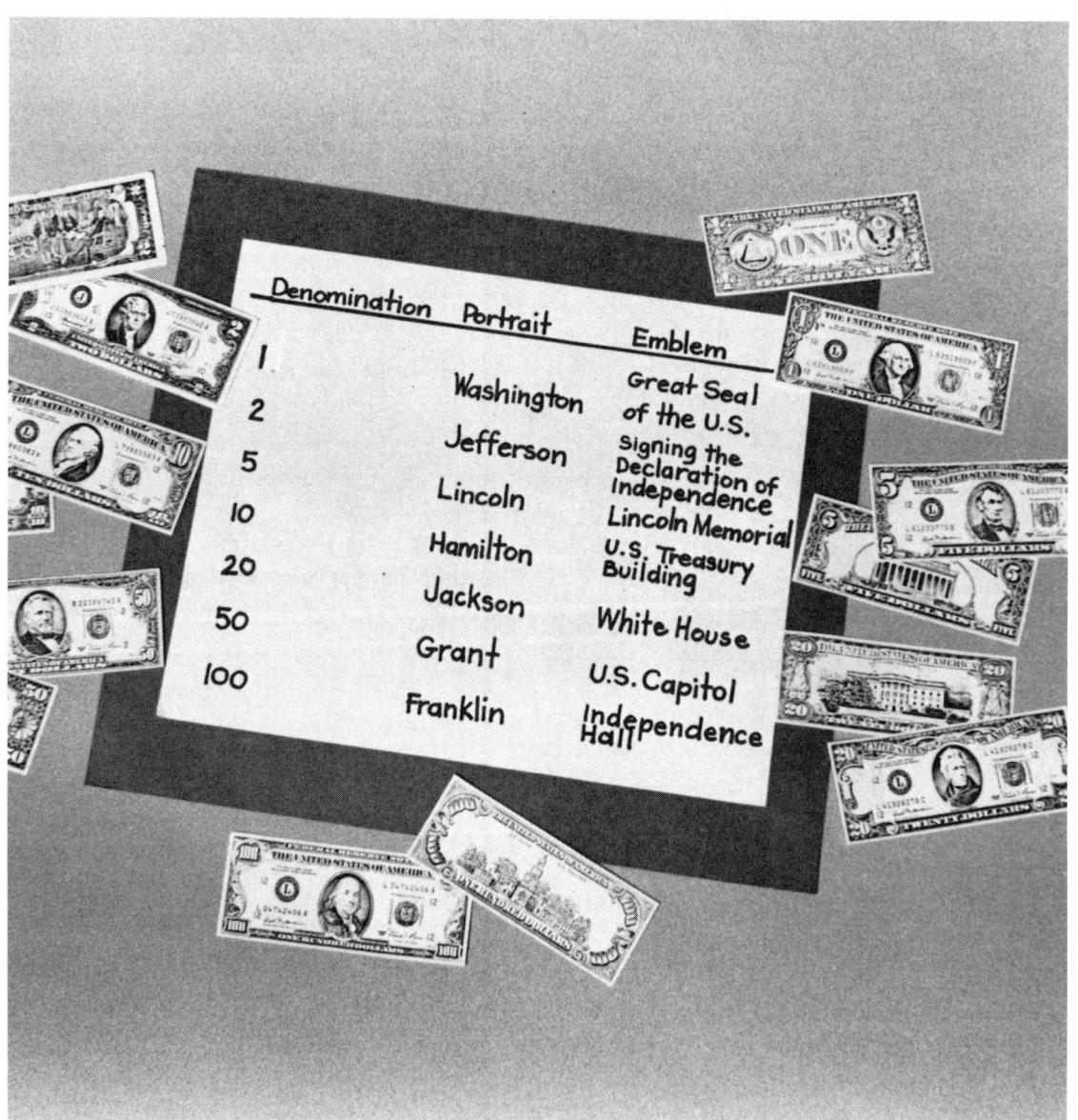

Objectives	Recognizing seven bills in circulation in the U.S. economy; learning American history, our important leaders and public servants, and U.S. emblems.
Activity	Copy five sets of facsimiles of the fronts of 1-, 2-, 5-, 10-, 20-, 50-, and 100-dollar bills (use the blackline master in the appendix). Divide the class into five groups. Give each group one set. Instruct each child to mark the numbers 1, 2, 5, 10, 20, 50, and 100 down the left column of a sheet of paper. Instruct the children to write out the names of the leaders on each of the dollar denominations on their paper. They will find these names under the portraits in the center of the bill. After you check their answers, review the history of each leader. Repeat the exercise with copies of the backs of the bills. This time children must identify the emblem in the center of the bill. After checking children's answers, review the importance of each emblem in our history. (Student sheets should look like the chart below)

Denomination	Portrait	Emblem
1	Washington	Great Seal of the U.S.
2	Jefferson	Signing the Declaration of Independence
5	Lincoln	Lincoln Memorial
10	Hamilton	U.S. Treasury Building
20	Jackson	White House
50	Grant	U.S. Capitol
100	Franklin	Independence Hall

Getting Started	The teacher might say, "Did you ever notice that each denomination of dollar has a portrait of a famous American? We will learn the different dollars by the pictures on them. Each bill has a portrait on the front and an emblem of the U.S. on the back." Start the exercise.
Follow-up Discussion	Washington was our first president, and is on the $ _____ bill. Which two bills have a portrait of someone who was not a U.S. president? Why is it important that we know exactly what each bill looks like? Who are the five presidents on the bills with pictures of presidents? Tell the class that Presidents McKinley, Cleveland, and Madison, and Chief Justice Chase are on the 500-, 1000-, 5000-, and 10,000-dollar bills, respectively.
Materials	Copier. Paper. Pencils. Blackline master for 1-, 2-, 5-, 10-, 20-, 50-, and 100-dollar bills.

4 Spending a Dollar

134   Money and the Bank

Objectives	Using basic math skills to determine how a dollar can be spent; learning the concept of scarcity.
Activity	Provide each child with a dollar's worth of change in play money. Each child should have the equivalent of five dimes, ten pennies, three nickels, and one quarter. Set up five boxes in front of the class. One box should contain pencils and have one pencil taped to the front of the box, where it is marked 5¢. Use the same procedure for the other four boxes, with erasers for 2¢, pens for 25¢, chalk for 5¢, and marbles for 10¢. Assign one student to each box. These students will have to collect the money for their items and keep a receipt. They should accept only the exact change for their items. Instruct the class to spend their dollars. Each child is told to buy at least one of each item. At their seats the children write a list of what they have bought with the price of each, showing a total of one dollar spent. Children selling the items should add up their receipts for the teacher. Children then may return the items for refunds.
Getting Started	The teacher might say, "Here is a dollar in change, using play money. I want everyone to first show me 'quarters.' Let me see your 'dimes.' Let me see your 'pennies.' Now, let me see your 'nickels.' Look at the boxes in front of the class. We are going to go shopping in class. Five of you will be sales-people and the rest will be shoppers. Each must buy at least one item from each box. You must use exact change when buying items." Start the exercise.
Follow-up Discussion	Do the exercise with other denominations of coins and bills. Why did each of you choose a different marketbasket of goods? Why is it often difficult to choose? Explain that both money and goods are scarce. Relate why prices tell us about the value of goods. Reinforce the idea that money must be spent wisely.
Materials	Erasers. Marbles. Pencils. Pens. Chalk. Five cigar boxes or shoeboxes. Tape. Marking pen. Blackline master for quarters, dimes, nickels, and pennies.

5 Money Math

Objectives   Learning to add and subtract using coins; understanding the relative values of a penny, nickel, dime, quarter, half-dollar, and one-dollar coin; recognizing the differences among coins.

Activity   Write on the chalkboard, *one penny = 1¢, one nickel = 5¢, one dime = 10¢, one quarter = 25¢, one half-dollar = 50¢,* and *one dollar = 100¢*. Divide the class

136   Money and the Bank

into four groups. Give each group the equivalent of 100 pennies, 20 nickels, 10 dimes, 1 half-dollar, and 1 dollar coin. Each group should choose a leader who will record the answers to the following questions on the chalkboard.

5 pennies = _____ nickel
10 pennies = _____ nickels or _____ dime
15 pennies = _____ nickels
20 pennies = _____ nickels or _____ dimes
25 pennies = _____ nickels or _____ quarter
30 pennies = _____ nickels or _____ dimes
35 pennies = _____ nickels
40 pennies = _____ nickels or _____ dimes
45 pennies = _____ nickels
50 pennies = _____ dimes or _____ half-dollar
55 pennies = _____ nickels
60 pennies = _____ dimes
65 pennies = _____ nickels
70 pennies = _____ dimes
75 pennies = _____ nickels or _____ quarters
80 pennies = _____ dimes
85 pennies = _____ nickels
90 pennies = _____ dimes
100 pennies = _____ dimes or _____ quarters or _____ dollar

Encourage the class to use the coins to count out the answers. Visit each group to facilitate the activity. Have group leaders compare answers with other group leaders and report back to their groups. Collect all money and all papers.

Getting Started

The teacher might say, "We are going to learn to use math the way we will be using it every day. We will count 'coins.' I will divide the class into four groups. Each group should choose a discussion leader. The leader will write the answers to the questions on the chalkboard. The whole group must work on each answer by counting out coins." Start the exercise.

Follow-up Discussion

Put a list of subtraction questions on the blackboard.
e.g., quarter − dime = __(15)__ ¢

Put a list of addition questions on the blackboard.
e.g., quarter + dime = __(35)__ ¢

Put a list of division questions on the blackboard.
e.g., quarter ÷ nickel = __(5)__ ¢

Put a list of multiplication questions on the blackboard.
e.g., 5 × quarter = $ __(1.25)__

Materials

Blackline masters for pennies, quarters, dimes, half-dollars and 1 dollar coin.
Chalk.
Chalkboard.

6 Heads — You Win!

138 Money and the Bank

Objectives	Recognizing coins and famous U.S. historical figures.
Activity	Set up five work stations in the classroom. Place one dime, one penny, one nickel, one quarter, one half-dollar, and one dollar coin play money (made from the blackline masters in the appendix) at each work station. Leave a space at each work station for 3" × 5" cards. The cards should be numbered with the following information:

(1) Lincoln	(12) 10¢	(23) In God We Trust
(2) Washington	(13) Liberty	(24) In God We Trust
(3) Anthony	(14) Liberty	(25) Most valuable
(4) Kennedy	(15) Liberty	(26) Least valuable
(5) Jefferson	(16) Liberty	(27) President
(6) Roosevelt	(17) Liberty	(28) President
(7) 1¢	(18) Liberty	(29) President
(8) 25¢	(19) In God We Trust	(30) President
(9) 100¢	(20) In God We Trust	(31) President
(10) 50¢	(21) In God We Trust	(32) Women's rights leader
(11) 5¢	(22) In God We Trust	

Cards are to be shuffled and distributed evenly to students at each work station. Children should place their cards in front of the coin they describe. Cards should be placed facing up in front of the coins so students will not place two of the same card in front of one coin. Visit with each group to facilitate the exercise. Reshuffle the cards and have groups do the exercise again until they get all cards placed properly.

Getting Started	"Each coin has a picture or a head on one side. These are heads of famous people in our history. Five of our coins show presidents of the United States and one of our coins shows a women's rights leader. We are going to play a matching game. The game will teach us who these people were." Start the exercise.
Follow-up Discussion	Repeat the exercise with either simpler or more difficult questions about the figures on each coin. Explain how the size of the coin does not relate to its value. Explain that learning the figures on each coin can help identify it.
Materials	3" × 5" index cards. Marking pen. Five copies of each of the following: pennies, nickels, dimes, quarters, half-dollars, and dollar coins (made from blackline masters).

7 Dogs

Objectives	Understanding the concept of bartering goods and services for other goods and services; learning that barter is an alternative to a price system for economic exchange.
Activity	The following exercise should be adjusted to your class size. A class of twenty-five would be divided into five groups of five children. Each group will be responsible for making five paper dogs. Give each group paste or tape to assemble the dogs. Distribute dog parts so that group 1 gets three tails, twenty legs, five bodies, and three heads; group 2 gets seven tails, twenty legs, three bodies, and five heads; group 3 gets five tails, twenty legs, seven bodies, and four heads; group 4 gets five tails, twenty legs, five bodies, and six heads; group 5 gets five tails, twenty legs, five bodies, and seven heads. One of the children in each group is responsible for one of the dog parts. The remaining child will collect all parts when the group has enough parts to assemble five dogs, each having one head, four legs, a body, and a tail. Each child in each group will assemble his or her own dog when all the necessary parts are gathered. Groups must barter with each other to obtain the necessary parts. It should be noted that this "free" trade among groups benefited all the groups. It should also be stressed that trade can be carried on without money through barter.
Getting Started	The teacher might say, "We are going to make dogs. Each dog will need one head, one body, one tail, and four legs. (Divide the class into groups.) Each group has an assortment of parts. Each child in a group should collect all of one kind of part. See if you have enough for five dogs. If not, trade with the other groups for parts. One in each group should collect all the parts, and then each of you will tape together your own dog. All finished dogs go to the dog pound in front of the class." Start the exercise.
Follow-up Discussion	Was barter easy? Would items with prices have made it easier to trade goods? Have you ever traded this way before? Try the exercise again but with play money so goods can be purchased. Try the game again, timing the groups for a winner.
Materials	Glue or tape for each group. Colored paper. Scissors. Marking pen. Ruler.

Money and the Bank   141

8 Barter/Trade

Objectives	Understanding that barter is a way of exchanging goods and services; creating a marketplace in a classroom where goods and services are traded by barter; learning that money is an easier and more efficient medium of exchange than barter.
Activity	Make five 2" × 2" cards for each child. Each set of cards should include one card labeled *food* with a picture of a hot dog, one card labeled *clothing* with a picture of a jacket, one card labeled *shelter* with a picture of a house, one card labeled *transportation* with a picture of a car, and the last card labeled *fun* with a picture of a movie ticket. Put together all the sets of cards and thoroughly shuffle them. Randomly give each child five cards. Children are to barter with each other until they have one card of each type. Time the class in this exercise. Repeat the same activity, but this time add a sixth card labeled *money* with a picture of a dollar bill. After shuffling the cards, give children six cards randomly instead of five. The money cards can be traded for any other. Children need to get only five cards, as before. Time the class exercise. Explain why the money card was an extra advantage. Explain why money acts in the economy to exchange goods and services more efficiently.
Getting Started	The teacher might say, "Each of us needs basic things. We all need food to eat. We all need a place to sleep. We need clothing to keep us warmer in the winter and cooler in the summer. We all need a way to be taken from place to place over a long distance. Lastly, it is also good if we can have some fun. We are going to play a trading game so each of us can have one of each of the things I mentioned." Start the exercise.
Follow-up Discussion	Why do we trade for goods and services? Why is money used to trade? How is money earned? Have you ever used money to trade? Have you ever bartered in a trade? Why is money of advantage in a trade? Why is money a medium of exchange?
Materials	Tagboard. Scissors. Glue. Marking pen. Pictures from magazines and newspapers.

9 Vegetable Money

144 Money and the Bank

Objectives	Learning how to buy things; learning basic addition skills; trading with money for goods; learning that money is a unit of account as well as a medium of exchange.
Activity	Instruct each child in the class in advance to bring in one or two empty cans of vegetables from home and a shopping list of one or two other cans of vegetables to "buy." Each can must be marked with a price. When the children bring the cans to class, pay for them with play coin money. Make sure each child has enough money to make change. Place all the cans in front of the class. In turn, let children do their shopping, go back to their seats, add up what they owe, and pay you (the cashier). Discuss the exercise. Allow students to bring their purchases and checklists home.
Getting Started	The teacher might say, "We are going to make a canned-vegetable store in class. I have put all your cans up here. Each one has a price. Look at your shopping list and buy the ones you need. At your seat add up how much you owe and pay me." Start the exercise.
Follow-up Discussion	Why did we trade with money? Why do we use different kinds of coins? Do you have enough money to buy all the items on your list? Why are math skills important to a consumer? Why do different vegetables have different prices? Repeat the exercise with different items. Introduce dollar bills in the same exercise.
Materials	Blackline masters for coins. Empty cans of vegetables. Paper. Pencils.

10 The Bank

Objectives	Learning that banks hold money for consumers, businesses, and the government; learning that banks pay us interest for the use of our money; learning that money is a store of value as well as a unit of account and a medium of exchange; using basic math skills.
Activity	Give each child a 3" × 5" index card on which is written at the top *Bank Book*. Choose one child to be the banker. Each card should have columns for date, amount deposited, interest paid, and total. Each day give children an amount of play money up to fifty cents to deposit in the "bank." The banker should mark the cards, and you should sign each entry. Explain that funds in a local bank can pay dividends daily. Weekly put on the chalkboard how many cents of interest are paid per dollar of deposit. Show the students how they can calculate their interest (e.g., if the rate is 5 percent APR*, each week they will get about .1 percent interest, or 1/10 cent per dollar per week, or one cent every ten weeks). Have the students post their own interest; collect and check cards for the next week. Return all money with interest at the end of the term. Explain how the bank earns interest (to pay depositors) by lending depositors' money to people who want to buy things now. Depositors are people who want to spend their money later and should have more money later because they waited. Rotate the banker's job each week and have students make their deposits. You may also wish to explain that banks use part of the interest they earn to pay depositors and part of the interest they earn to run the bank and to pay the owners of the bank.
Getting Started	The teacher might say, "We are going to start a savings account right here in class. Each child can have one of these card bank books. I will choose one child to be the banker. Each day you can make a deposit of any amount from one to fifty cents. The banker will pay for the use of your money—we will call that your interest." Start the exercise.
Follow-up Discussion	Have a local banker come to class. You may get him or her to give you official bank books for each child. Why is saving important? Do you or your family save? Why are we paid interest? Who may want to borrow our money? Why are people willing to pay interest to use our money?
Materials	3" × 5" index cards. Marking pen. Play money made from blackline master.

*Annual Percentage Rate

Money and the Bank

11 Shopping Spree

Objectives Understanding that the prices of goods and services vary and that different places offer similar goods and services for sale at different prices, which may vary from day to day; understanding that the supply of goods and services and the demand for them determine the daily selling prices; learning basic shopping skills in order to more effectively participate in the marketplace.

148   Money and the Bank

Activity	Give a piece of tagboard to each child in the class. Assign one commonly used supermarket item to each child. Children write the names of their goods at the top of their pieces of tagboard, and they mark off a space for each class day for the next four weeks. The children hang their tagboards around the classroom. Each day they will check with their parents how much they are paying for their assigned goods and mark that price on their tagboards. If parents did not purchase the good the previous day, then have the children mark *NA* in that day's space on their tagboards. You may wish to assign two children the same good so they can see the different prices over time and at the same time. Mark the children's tagboards showing the change in price from week to week. Announce to the class those goods that have changed in price the most and the least.
Getting Started	The teacher might say, "Do you always pay the same amount for the things you buy? Do your parents always pay the same price for the things they buy? Why do prices change? Prices can change when we are willing to pay more or when we are willing to pay less. Prices are higher, for example, for an orange drink on the beach. Why? Because at the beach we are very thirsty and are willing to pay more. Prices also change when there is too much or too little of the things we want. For example, sellers with more orange drinks than they think they can sell would want to lower their prices to sell all their drinks. Today you are going to make posters so you can each follow the changes in the prices of goods our families buy." Start the exercise.
Follow-up Discussion	Are prices important? Why? What does the word *inflation* mean? What does the word *deflation* mean? Why does the fact that we may want something more make its price go up? Why does the fact that we may want a good or service less make its price go down? Are the prices of things different from place to place? Do the prices of things change over time? Why will sellers with more than they think they can sell lower their prices? Why will sellers with less than they think they can sell raise their prices? Can the time of year change a price? Can the location of a product change its price?
Materials	Tagboards. Marking pens. Examples of goods children are to find the prices of.

12 Money Math Is for Me!

Objectives	Learning to use basic math skills in a marketplace for goods and services; understanding that mathematics is very important in knowing how to buy and sell goods and services.
Activity	Show the class some commonly purchased items. Show the prices marked on each. Tell the class that math is needed to be able to know how much money is needed to buy or sell something. Duplicate and pass out Money Mystery Game sheets (see appendix). At their seats, children complete the exercise to find the mystery words.
Getting Started	The teacher might say, "We are going to play a game. I will pass out a sheet with a number of questions on it. Find the answer to each question and fill in the mystery words. You will learn that math is very important for finding out how to buy and sell goods and services." Start the exercise.
Follow-up Discussion	Why is math fun? Why is mathematics used to buy goods and services? Why is mathematics used to sell goods and services? Why is it very important to count your change when buying something? How can you be sure you paid the proper amount? How have you used math when buying and selling?
Materials	Paper. Pencils. Copier. Blackline master for Money Mystery Game (in the appendix).

13 Checks

Objectives	Learning that checks can be written to draw money out of an account at a bank or savings institution; learning that checks are used like money as a medium of exchange; understanding and using basic math skills.
Activity	Lesson 13 can be done while the activity in Lesson 10 is going on and when children have built up a few dollars in their accounts. Copy checks that have a place for an amount to be written out in words and in numbers, a space to write *Pay to the order of,* and spaces for purpose, check number, signature, and date. Have each child practice writing a check for twenty-five cents. The class banker will record the transactions in the students' bank books, stamp the checks *PAID* when they are recorded, and return the checks to the children.
Getting Started	The teacher might say, "Did you ever see your mother or father pay for a good or service with a check? Was the check as good as money? Checks are ways of giving a person money from your bank account. The person takes your check because he or she knows it can be given to your bank for the money it represents. We are going to use checks in class." Start the exercise.
Follow-up Discussion	Were checks easier to use than money? What happens when you lose a check? Why is losing a check different from losing money? Why are checks accepted like money? How can you be sure the bank has paid for the checks you write? How do you pay a bank for the service of keeping a checking account for you?
Materials	Paper. Copier. Bank books from Lesson 10.

14 Green Card, Red Card

154   Money and the Bank

Objectives	Learning that prices determine the relative values of goods and services; understanding that every good or service has a price; using money as a medium of exchange to purchase goods and services.
Activity	Make sixty 5″ × 7″ cards out of green paper and sixty 5″ × 7″ cards out of red paper. Write on the green cards the name of the person or persons who are buying (for example, on the green cards you might write: "Judy bought," "the family bought," "the store owner bought," or "the teacher bought"). Each of the sentence fragments on a green card should be completed on a red card. For example, the red cards might read: "a dress for $20," "a new car for $5000," "a cash register for $600," or "a ruler for 50¢." As you can see, the four examples for the green cards match the four examples for the red cards. This procedure should be done to all sixty sets of cards. Divide the class into four groups. Divide the cards into four groups so that each group has fifteen red cards that match fifteen green cards. Give each group a shuffled group of cards. Have the groups match up all their cards. Each time a red card is matched correctly with a green card they should be turned in to the teacher. The group that turns in its cards first wins.
Getting Started	The teacher might say, "I am going to divide the class into four groups. Each group will get fifteen red and fifteen green cards. The red cards are for price and the green cards are for people. Together one green and one red card completes a sentence about the purchase of a good or service. Groups will match their green and red cards and turn in completed sets to me. The first group to turn in all its cards wins." Start the exercise.
Follow-up Discussion	Why have prices for goods and services? Do we always pay the same price for the things we buy? How do you know you paid a fair price? How do you know you found a "bargain"? Do you or your friends talk about prices? Do members of your family talk about prices? Why is it a good idea to shop for the best prices?
Materials	Red paper. Green paper. Marking pen. Scissors.

15 Crayon Money

156　Money and the Bank

Objectives	Understanding that the amount or supply of money in the economy changes the prices of goods and services; learning that an increase in the supply of money can raise prices and a decrease in the supply of money can lower prices of goods and services we buy.
Activity	Suddenly announce on a given day that a whole crayon is worth one box of raisins. Sell raisins for crayons. Make sure you have enough raisins so all those who wish to buy can do so. Announce that tomorrow you will trade raisins for crayons again. On the second day bring to class the same amount of raisins as you sold on the first day. Sell all your raisins. Make sure that at least *twice* the number of crayons are available today. Tell the class that due to an increase in money or crayons the price of raisins will rise to two crayons. Trade at the new rate during the next class. Discuss with the class why crayons were a poor substitute for money after the first day. Show the children that when they were allowed to have as much money as they liked by using more crayons, the price rose. Explain to the class that money can be increased as well to cause higher prices for goods and services. Explain that in general it is the responsibility of government to be sure the right amount of money is put in circulation so prices will not go too low or too high.
Getting Started	The teacher might say, "Today I will sell a box of raisins for one whole crayon. After I have sold raisins to all who wish to buy them we will return to today's other activities." Announce at the end of the day that you will allow crayons to be used like money the very next day for raisins. After all your raisins are sold out, announce the price increase. Explain that prices go up when the supply of money or crayons for money goes up. Explain that there are not enough raisins for all who wish to buy raisins at the current price and that by raising prices you can be sure only those who can afford to buy raisins will do so. This way you can get more crayons, and the supply of raisins can match the demand for them. Start the exercise.
Follow-up Discussion	Why did I run out of raisins the second day? Why did we end up with too much crayon money? How can more crayon money cause higher prices for raisins? How can the supply of money change prices? Why is it important to limit the amount of money? Could less money cause prices to fall?
Materials	Small boxes of raisins. Crayons.

16 Money Madness

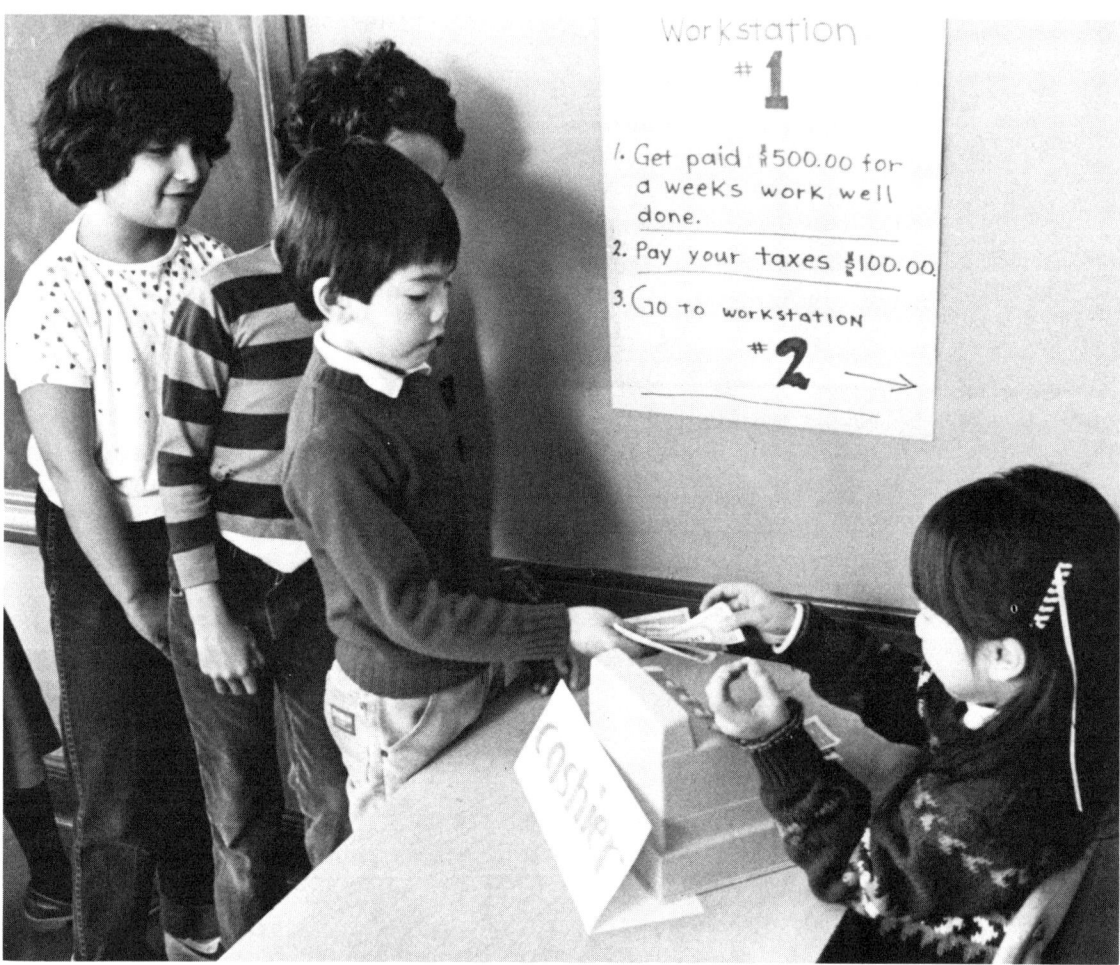

Objectives Using basic math skills to earn, save, and spend money; learning how to transact the purchases of goods and services and to make change; understanding the use of money as a unit of account.

Activity Set up the following series of ten work stations. Each work station should have enough play money for the children to make change. Play money in 1-, 5-, 10-, 20-, 50-, and 100-dollar denominations is used. Work station 1:

158   Money and the Bank

Display a poster that reads, "Get paid $500 for a week's work well done. Pay your taxes—$100—and go to work station 2." Work station 2: Display a poster that reads, "Pay the doctor $50 for fixing your bad back. You get paid $5 an hour for the last three hours you worked late. Go to work station 3." Work station 3: Display a poster that reads, "Win $35 playing 'Bingo'! Go to work station 4." Work station 4: Display a poster that reads, "Pay 10 percent of your money to build a better school. Go to work station 5." Work station 5: Display a poster that reads, "Pay $160 to Banana Travel for a vacation in Banana Land. Go to work station 6." Work station 6: Display a poster that reads, "Pay $5 to go to the movies. Pay $10 for a new skateboard. Pay $3 for a pen. Pay $12 for a book. Go to work station 7." Work station 7: Display a poster that reads, "Get paid $10 for mowing the neighbor's lawn. Go to work station 8." Work station 8: Display a poster that reads,"Receive a stock dividend of $115. Go to work station 9." Work station 9: Display a poster that reads, "Double your money at the sweepstakes! Go to work station 10." Work station 10: "Pay off the $100 loan you made for a bicycle. Turn in your remaining cash to the teacher."

Have children turn in their money without others seeing how much they turned in. All children who turn in any amount other than $490 must go through the series of work stations again. Place enough play money at each work station for the class.

Getting Started	The teacher might say, "You will go to the first work station one at a time. Follow the directions at each work station. When you are finished, give me the money you have. Don't let anyone know how much you turn in. Those who turn in the wrong amount at the end must go through each of the work stations again." Start the exercise.
Follow-up Discussion	Why is it important to count change carefully? Do you ever use money in the same way as we did in class? Why is math so important in economics? Why do we use money as a medium of exchange? Why do we use money as a unit of account? Why do we use money as a store of value? Why was this activity an example of using money as a unit of account?
Materials	Play money in 1-, 5-, 10-, 20-, 50-, and 100-dollar denominations made from the blackline master. Posters. Tape. Marking pen.

17 Make a Deal

Objectives Learning to participate in the marketplace; learning how the supply of a good or service and the demand for a good or service determine its price. (Show that demand is greater when the price is lower and that demand is less when the price is higher. Show that supply is greater when the price is higher and supply is less when the price is lower. Show that equilibrium price is where the supply price and the demand price are equal. The market clears at the equilibrium price. Equilibrium prices are determined by both the supply and the demand.)

Activity Make forty-eight 3" × 5" cards (twenty-four green buyer cards and twenty-four red seller cards). The buyer cards should read as follows: four read "buy at less than 10¢," four read "buy at less than 9¢," four read "buy at less than 8¢," four read "buy at less than 7¢," four read "buy at less than

6¢," and four read "buy at less than 5¢." The seller cards should read as follows: four read "sell at more than 4¢," four read "sell at more than 5¢," four read "sell at more than 6¢," four read "sell at more than 7¢," four read "sell at more than 8¢," and four read "sell at more than 9¢." Divide the class in half. Instruct one-half of the class to be buyers and one-half to be sellers. Buyers take buyer cards and sellers take seller cards one at a time from shuffled piles that are face down. One buyer and one seller must agree on a price and return their cards to you. Each has three chances to make a transaction. If they are unable to make a transaction, the card may be returned and placed at the bottom of its deck, and a new card is issued.

Children are encouraged to make as many transactions as possible. All transactions are recorded on the chalkboard. Allow the game to proceed for thirty minutes. Collect all cards. Explain why buyers seek lower prices and sellers seek higher prices. Show that together buyers and sellers determine prices in a marketplace like you had in class that day. You can make the game more interesting by introducing a product to the game.

Getting Started	The teacher might say, "I am going to divide the class into two groups. One group will be sellers. The other group will be buyers, and they are going to buy from the sellers. Buyers will pick one card from the buyers' deck. Sellers will pick one card from the sellers' deck. Each child has three chances to buy or sell at an agreed price. When buyers and sellers agree on a price, return your cards to me and get another one. You should try to make as many sales or purchases as you can. I will keep track of all sales and purchases on the chalkboard." Explain the exercise and the concept skills. Show how prices were determined by supply and demand in the marketplace.
Follow-up Discussion	Why do buyers want to pay a lower price? Why do sellers want to get a higher price? How do buyers and sellers determine prices? How was our class a marketplace today? What might happen if there were many more buyers than sellers? What might happen if there were many more sellers than buyers? Why can we say that the buyers create the demand? Why can we say that the sellers create the supply? Try the game again, but make more buyers than sellers, and show the class how prices rise. Try the game again, but make more sellers than buyers, and show the class how prices fall.
Materials	Green paper. Red paper. Scissors. Chalkboard. Chalk. Marking pen.

18 Why Prices?

Objectives Learning that money is a medium of exchange; learning that prices determine the value of goods and services and that prices determine how goods and services are distributed in our economy; learning the concepts of supply, demand, producer, and consumer.

Activity Prepare five buyer cards on 3″ × 5″ green paper as follows. Card 1: oranges (on the front) and "I am thirsty!" (on the back). Card 2: bananas (on the front) and "They make me sick!" (on the back). Card 3: chewing gum (on the front) and "It gives me cavities." (on the back). Card 4: ice skates (on the front) and "I have a new skating rink to go to." (on the back). Card 5: lollipop (on the front) and "My parents told me not to eat them." (on the

162 Money and the Bank

back). Prepare five seller cards on 3″ × 5″ red paper as follows. Card 6: oranges (on the front) and "They are hard to find." (on the back). Card 7: bananas (on the front) and "They are easy to find." (on the back). Card 8: chewing gum (on the front) and "I can buy them for less money now." (on the back). Card 9: ice skates (on the front) and "They are hard to make." (on the back). Card 10: lollipop (on the front) and "I have only one left." (on the back). Divide the class into five groups of buyers and five groups of sellers. Give each buying group one buyers' card and each selling group one sellers' card. Give the groups about five minutes to read and discuss their cards. Tell them that the statements on the backs of the cards indicate whether they are to increase or decrease their prices.

Turn the ten groups into five groups by putting the buyers and sellers of the same products together. Give them ten minutes to discuss prices. Explain why children who are either buyers or sellers of oranges, bananas, chewing gum, or ice skates agree on increasing or decreasing their prices but the buyers and sellers of lollipops disagree. The buyers should agree to pay less for lollipops because their parents told them not to eat them, and the sellers want a higher price because there is only one lollipop left. (*Note:* Orange prices should rise, banana prices should fall, chewing gum prices should fall, ice skate prices should rise, and lollipop prices should be undecided.)

Getting Started

The teacher might say, "I will divide the class into ten groups. Five groups will be buyers and five groups will be sellers. Each group will have one card. The front of the card tells you what it is you are buying or selling. The back of the card tells you if you should ask for or pay a higher or lower price. Later I will bring the buyers and the sellers together to discuss pricing." Start the exercise.

Follow-up Discussion

Why do goods and services have prices?
Why do some things cost more and some things less?
Did you ever want something but not have enough money to buy it?
Have you ever seen sellers lower their prices when people could not afford the products they were selling?
Why did some class sellers lower prices?
Why did some of the class sellers raise prices?
Why did some buyers offer higher prices?
Why did some buyers offer lower prices?
When is a seller called a producer?
When is a buyer called a consumer?
How do producers and consumers together determine prices?

Materials

Green 3″ × 5″ cards.
Red 3″ × 5″ cards.
Marking pen.
Chalk.
Chalkboard.

Money and the Bank 163

19 Around the World

Objectives	Using basic mathematics skills in spending, earning, and saving money.
Activity	Prepare 3″ × 5″ cards in three categories: spending, earning, and saving. Examples of what is to be written on spending cards are: I bought 2 donuts at 20¢ each for _____ ¢; I bought 5 cards at 10¢ each for _____ ¢; I bought 12 rubber bands for _____ ¢, because they cost 1¢ each; If donuts cost 30¢ and milk 50¢, then 2 donuts and milk cost _____ ¢. Examples of what is to be written on earning cards are: If I worked for $1 per hour, I would get _____ dollars for 3 hours' work; If I hired someone to shovel the snow off my driveway for $2 and it took one hour, they would make _____ dollars per hour; It would cost me how much to hire 5 workers for an hour at $1.50 per hour for each? Examples of what is written on the savings cards are: If I save $1 for one year and get 10 percent interest, I will get _____ ¢ per year in interest; If I save $100 at 10 percent interest for one year, I will get _____ dollars interest per year; If I save 5¢ per day for 10 days, then I will have saved _____ ¢.

You can make as many cards as you feel your class can handle in one day. Create other questions that fit the level of your class. Have the entire class stand. Give a card to each child. Have children pair off. In turn, each will ask the other the question on her or his card. Give each child a chance to ask a question. When children answer incorrectly have them give you their cards and be seated. After one round give one of your cards to each of the remaining children standing. Repeat the exercise until only three children remain standing. They get the buyer, saver, and earner awards. |
Getting Started	The teacher might say, "I will give cards to each of you. Now stand. We are going to play 'Around the World.' The world is the classroom and each of you will get to ask the other a question on your card until we go around the entire room. Students who answer the question incorrectly will sit down; return those questions to me, and I will use them later. The last three children left standing get the best earner, best saver, and best spender awards." Start the exercise.
Follow-up Discussion	Why is it important to use math skills when we spend money? Why is it important to use math skills when we earn money? Why is it important to use math skills when we save money?
Materials	3″ × 5″ cards. Marking pen.

20 Jobs and Money

166   Money and the Bank

Objectives	Using basic math skills used in daily life; understanding that most income in the United States is earned from wages and salaries; learning to associate the wages and salaries made with the expenses of an average household.
Activity	List on the chalkboard the following jobs and salaries. *Plumber—$450 per week, Physician—$800 per week, Gardener—$250 per week, Secretary—$200 per week, Firefighter—$395 per week,* and *Pilot—$750 per week.* Divide the class into six groups. Give each of the groups one of the jobs listed. Provide each with a salary check and a stub indicating deductions for FICA (Federal Insurance Corporation of America, or Social Security)—take 7 percent, Federal withholding tax (take 20 percent), state income tax (take 10 percent), and withholding for health and life insurance (take 10 percent). Have each group determine its net pay or pay after deductions. Give each group the following bills: rent—$50, electricity—$5, phone—$2, gasoline—$5, food—$25, and clothing—$5. Have each group determine how much of the remaining salary it would spend or save. Have each group turn in a sheet of paper listing job, salary, net salary, salary after expenses, savings, and remaining income to be spent.
Getting Started	The teacher might say, "Each of you is going to have a job. You will be paid. When you get paid you will have to pay your taxes and expenses. You will find out what expenses your families have. You will decide what to do with money you have left. You will learn about decisions parents have to make." Start the exercise.
Follow-up Discussion	For higher grade levels, make the jobs, salaries, and deductions more difficult. Increase the number and complexity of the expenses for more advanced children. Discuss with the class the problems that arise at home when bills must be paid. Discuss with the class some of the actual bills their families have. Have children bring in old, already paid bills from their homes to use in the exercise.
Materials	Paper. Pencils. Chalk. Chalkboard. Copier.

GLOSSARY

This glossary contains many of the key terms and concepts found in this book. Terms and concepts have been defined so each can be explained more easily to young children.

B

bank A place where people keep their money for safety and to earn interest. Banks use this money to make loans.

barter Exchanging goods or services for each other.

business A place where people buy goods or services. A business can also be a place where goods are made or services provided. A business such as a store or a factory can be owned by one person or a group of people.

C

capital One of the factors of production. Capital is the building and what is in the building to make either goods or services. Capital can also be the money business needs to get started or to get bigger.

check A piece of paper that can be used at a store or bank for money—it is a written order to a bank to pay the stated amount of money from one's account.

coins Money made of metal. Coins in our country are pennies, nickels, dimes, quarters, half-dollars, and one dollar coins. Coins are made and controlled by the United States Treasury.

competition More than one business selling a similar good or service. Each tries to get more customers than the other.

consumer A person who buys a good or service from a business.

D

demand The amount of a good or service a consumer will buy at different prices.

durable good A good that will last for at least one year.

E

economics The study of how people try to get the most and make the most from what they have. Economics teaches how to earn, work, and spend better. Economics is also the study of how governments can be run.

exchange Giving up either money or a good or service for a different good or service.

F

factors What is needed to produce goods or services. The four factors of production are land, labor, capital, and management.

federal reserve notes United States currency or dollar bills—paper money printed by the United States Treasury but controlled by the Federal Reserve Bank of the United States. Federal Reserve Note denominations are one-dollar, two-dollar, five-dollar, ten-dollar, twenty-dollar, fifty-dollar, one-hundred dollar bills, as well as some larger denominations.

G

goods Products made or sold by businesses. Governments also make goods.

government A group of people making rules for all people in a country. They make rules about the economy and on how people can do business. Many goods and services come from government.

H

human capital Education and training to become a better worker.

I

inflation A rise in the general prices of goods and services.

J

job Making either a good or doing a service for money.

L

labor Workers who make goods and provide services. Labor is one of the factors of production.

M

management People who get labor, land, and capital together to make goods and services. Management is one of the factors of production.

market Any place where buyers and sellers of goods or services come together.

medium of exchange Something used to buy a good or a service.

money Anything commonly accepted in exchange for a good or service. In the United States, coins, Federal Reserve Notes, and checks are used the most to buy goods and services.

money supply The amount of money in the country that can be used to buy goods or services.

N

necessity Goods or services that are needed to stay alive. Food, clothing, and shelter are necessities.

nondurable good A good that usually will last less than a year.

nonrenewable resource Something that comes from land and cannot be replaced. Oil is an example of a nonrenewable resource.

P

price Amount that is needed to buy a good or service.

producer A person or group of people who make a good or a service.

production How goods or services are made.

professional A person who has special abilities in a job, or extensive education or training. Examples of professionals are physicians, teachers, and football players.

public sector That part of the economy where goods or services are made by workers who work for the government.

public service A job in government providing a service.

R

renewable resources Something that comes from land but can be replaced. Trees are an example of a renewable resource.

resource Any element in the environment; one of the factors of production.

S

savings Money put aside to be used later. Savings in a bank earns interest.

scarcity The situation where there is not enough goods or services for everyone all the time.

services Something that is done for another, such as fixing a car or mowing the grass. Businesses often provide services and are paid for them.

skilled labor Workers who have special abilities in making goods or services. Usually some special training or education is needed to become a skilled laborer. Carpenters and plumbers are examples of skilled laborers.

specialization Dividing up jobs in making a good or a service. Dividing up jobs usually makes producing the good or service easier and faster.

supply The amount of a good or service a producer will make at different prices.

T

taxes The money we pay to government, used in part to provide goods or services for all of us.

U

unions A group of workers asking to secure good economic conditions from their employers. Often one of the workers speaks for the group. Unions may ask for more pay or a better place to work.

unskilled labor Workers who have no special abilities in making goods or services. Delivering a newspaper or washing a dish is unskilled labor.

U.S. currency A Federal Reserve Note.

V

value The worth of a thing in money or goods that can be exchanged at a certain time.

W

wages The amount of money that is paid to labor for making goods and services.

BLACKLINE MASTERS

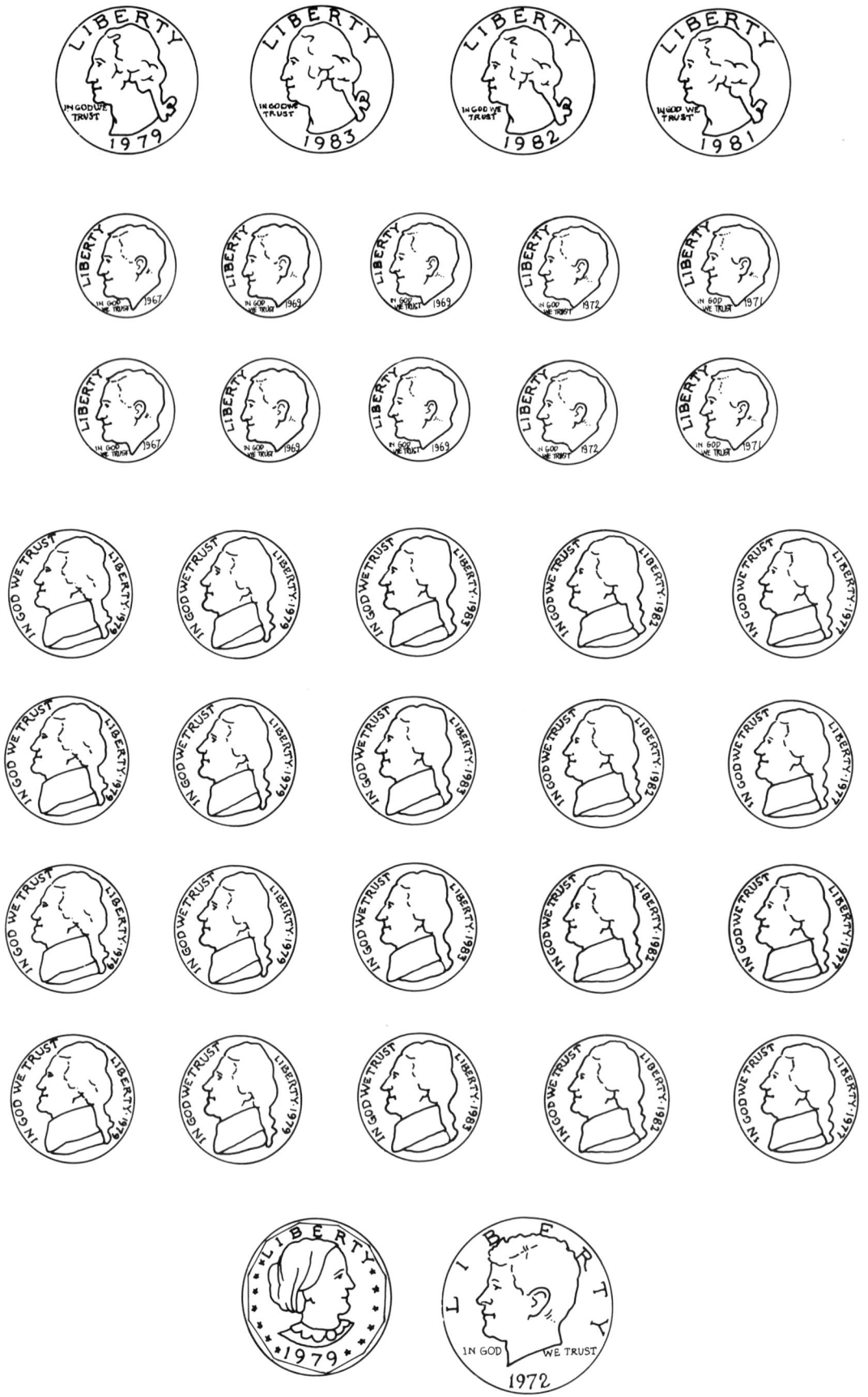

© 1985 by Addison-Wesley Publishing Company, Inc.

© 1985 by Addison-Wesley Publishing Company, Inc.

© 1985 by Addison-Wesley Publishing Company, Inc.

© 1985 by Addison-Wesley Publishing Company, Inc.

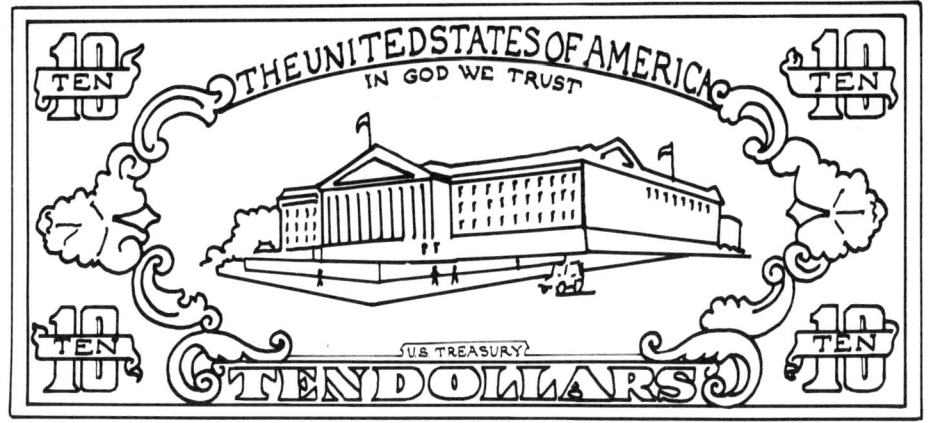
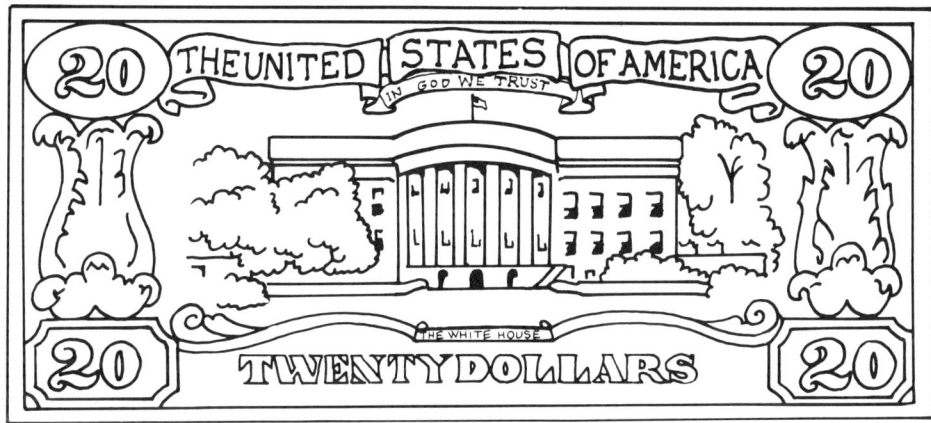

© 1985 by Addison-Wesley Publishing Company, Inc.

MONEY MYSTERY GAME

Directions:

Fill in the blanks. Use the codes to find the letter that goes with your answer. Fill in all the mystery words at the bottom of the page.

1. Four crayons at 1¢ each cost _____ ¢.
2. I can sell three pens for _____ ¢ each to get 30¢.
3. If apples cost 50¢, I can buy _____ for $1.50.
4. One apple for 50¢ and one orange for 50¢ cost _____ dollar(s) together.
5. _____ baseballs at 10¢ each cost 50¢.
6. _____ pencils cost 40¢ when they are 10¢ each.
7. If eight pairs of shoes cost $8.00, then two pairs of shoes cost _____ dollar(s).
8. My sister owes me five times more than a dime, or _____ ¢.
9. Two dollars equal _____ quarters.
10. My six pennies are worth _____ ¢.
11. Five nickels are worth _____ ¢.
12. Three quarters are worth _____ ¢.
13. Fifty apples at 20¢ each cost _____ dollar(s).
14. My dime is worth _____ ¢ less than your quarter.
15. One dollar equals _____ quarters.
16. Ten dimes equal _____ dollar(s).

Code

1	=	E
4	=	M
10	=	O
3	=	N
8	=	H
5	=	Y
25	=	S
75	=	F
50	=	T
2	=	A
6	=	I
15	=	R

___ ___ ___ ___ ___   ___ ___ ___ ___   ___ ___   ___ ___ ___   ___ ___
1 2 3 4 5   6 7 8 9   10 11   12 13 14   15 16

© 1985 by Addison-Wesley Publishing Company, Inc.